ALASKA AND THE YUKON

ALASKA AND THE YUKON

Photography
Brian Milne, Myron Wright
and many others

Essays and Tales
Larry Beck, Nan Elliot,
Lael Morgan, Jim Rearden,
Nancy Simmerman,
Lowell Thomas, Jr.

Andrew Hume,
Dick North,
Rhondda Snary

Facts On File Publications
460 Park Avenue South
New York, N.Y. 10016

Produced by Jürgen F. Boden
Designed by Hartmut Brückner

ALASKA AND THE YUKON

Published in the United States of America in 1983
by Facts on File, Inc., 460 Park Avenue South,
New York, N.Y. 10016

Copyright © 1983 by Jürgen F. Boden

All rights reserved. No part of this book may be reproduced or
utilized in any form or by any means, electronic or mechanical,
including photocopying, recording or by any information storage and
retrieval systems, without permission in writing from the Publisher.

ISBN 0-87196-813-4

Acknowledgements:

Alaska satellite picture by permission of U.S. Geological Survey,
Branch of Alaskan Geology, Menlo Park, California, U.S.A.

Yukon Territory satellite picture by permission of
National Air Photo Library, Ottawa, Canada.

Map of Alaska and the Yukon Territory: © Rand McNally & Company,
R.L. 83-S-58.

Excerpts from »The Collected Poems of Robert Service«
reprinted by permission of Dodd, Mead and Company, Inc.,
New York, N.Y., U.S.A.

Published simultaneously in the United States of America by
Facts on File, Inc., New York, in Canada by Collins Publishers,
Toronto, and in the Federal Republic of Germany by
Umschau Verlag, Frankfurt.

Lithographed, printed and bound in the Federal Republic of Germany
by Brönners Druckerei, Frankfurt.

Contents

Foreword by the editors

To visit Alaska the first time is a totally new and dramatic experience, quite different from what one might expect. With few exceptions, put aside what you have read or learned from television features about this last northern frontier. Anchorage, the »unofficial« capital, is the only place which does remind you that you are still in modern North America. Elsewhere, it is only the language and the neon signs. If you should cruise through the mellow rain-forest climate of Southeast Alaska and disembark in the charming state capital, Juneau, you can board a small northwest-bound jet to Anchorage and see below you the world's most breathtaking glacial arena: the Alaska-Yukon St. Elias Mountains and the Chugach Mountains, including, just after crossing Yakutat Bay, the Malaspina Glacier, North America's largest, at 1,120 sq. miles. This flight is perhaps the best introduction to the »real« Alaska.

Whether you travel on by road or by air you will soon begin to encounter the various features of this last wilderness in all their moods: the ·Wrangell Mountains with their crystal-clear rivers; the colorful Alaska Range with towering Mt. McKinley, North America's highest peak, trying to shelter Southcentral Alaska from the ruthless arctic winds; the massive Brooks Range, 250 miles north of »pioneer« city Fairbanks, its spurs reaching almost from the Yukon to the Chukchi Sea; the taiga and the tundra; the almost 350 sq. miles of Arctic sand dunes of the Kobuk Valley National Park; and the mighty Yukon River, meandering through Alaska from east to west. Finally there is the powerful man-made Trans-Alaska pipeline, punched through the land from north to south.

From the ice of the Arctic Ocean through the vicious storms of the Bering Sea you will approach the chain of the Aleutian Islands with their many active volcanoes, reaching out towards the Kamtschatka Peninsula of the U.S.S.R., and on whose most western island – Attu – the Japanese attempted to build their first military bridgehead on the North American continent in World War II.

And then there is Kodiak Island, mighty rock in the sea, green and flower-covered in summer, the second largest island under the U.S. flag (next to Hawaii) and of particular interest for being the home of the giant Kodiak brown bear.

The land of Alaska and the Yukon and their waters are home to an incredibly large and healthy population of mammals, birds and fish; indeed, even in the continuous permafrost regions north of the Arctic Circle, there is an abundance of animal life.

You will find any natural color in Alaska and the Yukon and in September, nature paints the land brilliantly red, yellow, brown and purple. In spring and fall, the night skies are brushed by the blues, greens, purples and reds of the rustling Aurora Borealis.

But even the most exciting landscape would be bleak indeed without the warmth and the ever-helping hand of one's neighbor and here a hard-working people, numbering about 420,000, exhibit the special kind of vitality and strength needed to withstand the harshest features of this last frontier. Alaska was purchased by the United States from Russia in 1867 for $7.2 million, a truly nominal amount measured against the value of oil, natural gas and minerals in this state which lost its territorial status to become the 49th star of the U.S. flag on January 3, 1959.

One interesting way to travel to the Yukon is via one of the ferries of the Alaska Marine Highway system which runs between Juneau and Skagway. Located at the northern end of the Lynn Canal, Skagway became famous in 1897, when thousands of fortune-seekers arrived there to fight their way through the Chilkoot Pass to the headwaters of the Yukon River, whence the long and dangerous journey by boat and raft to the Klondike gold fields began. Three years later, in 1900, the White Pass and Yukon Route railroad which had been built by courageous men using pick, shovel and dynamite was put into service. It would bring tens of thousands more adventurers and their equipment to Whitehorse, cutting a little shorter their trip to the northern gold fields around Dawson.

Today, you can re-live these times on a scenic eight-hour railway tour through canyons and tunnels to Whitehorse, the Yukon's capital, where about three quarters of the Territory's total population of 25,000 or so people live. And if you wish, you can drive on 330 miles to Dawson City where many surviving gold rush buildings have been preserved and restored. Here, you can catch the spirit of those days and even do your own gold panning.

The Yukon Territory is notable not only for its eventful history but also for geographical features. The Yukon's bone-chilling winter nights will recall for you Jack London's novels and the poems of Robert Service.

Today, the Territory subsists mainly on mining and tourism – both requisites for good roads. The network of highways in service now, most of them solidly built on gravel, is indeed a masterpiece of modern construction and has its crowning achievement in the 1979 completion of the Dempster Highway, one of the world's most northern. Stretching 460 miles from the Klondike River through the Ogilvie and Richardson Mountains to Inuvik in the Northwest Territories, where the Mackenzie River delta reaches the Beaufort Sea, the Dempster Highway carries with it some of the most chilling Arctic tales from Canada's north and travels through wilderness that once was the refuge of a real-life legend – »Albert Johnson« the so-called Mad Trapper.

We would like to express our gratitude, thanks and appreciation for helping us to produce this book to Mrs. Lael Morgan, Anchorage, to Mr. John Farnan, Juneau, to Mr. Tony Carson, Whitehorse, to our text editor Mr. Tim Jones, Alaska, who has long known and loved this last northern frontier, and last but not least to our book designer Hartmut Brückner.

Jürgen F. Boden
GROUP 4

ALASKA

Area: 586,000
square miles
Population:
420,000
State capital: Juneau
Tallest mountain:
Mt. McKinley,
20,320 feet

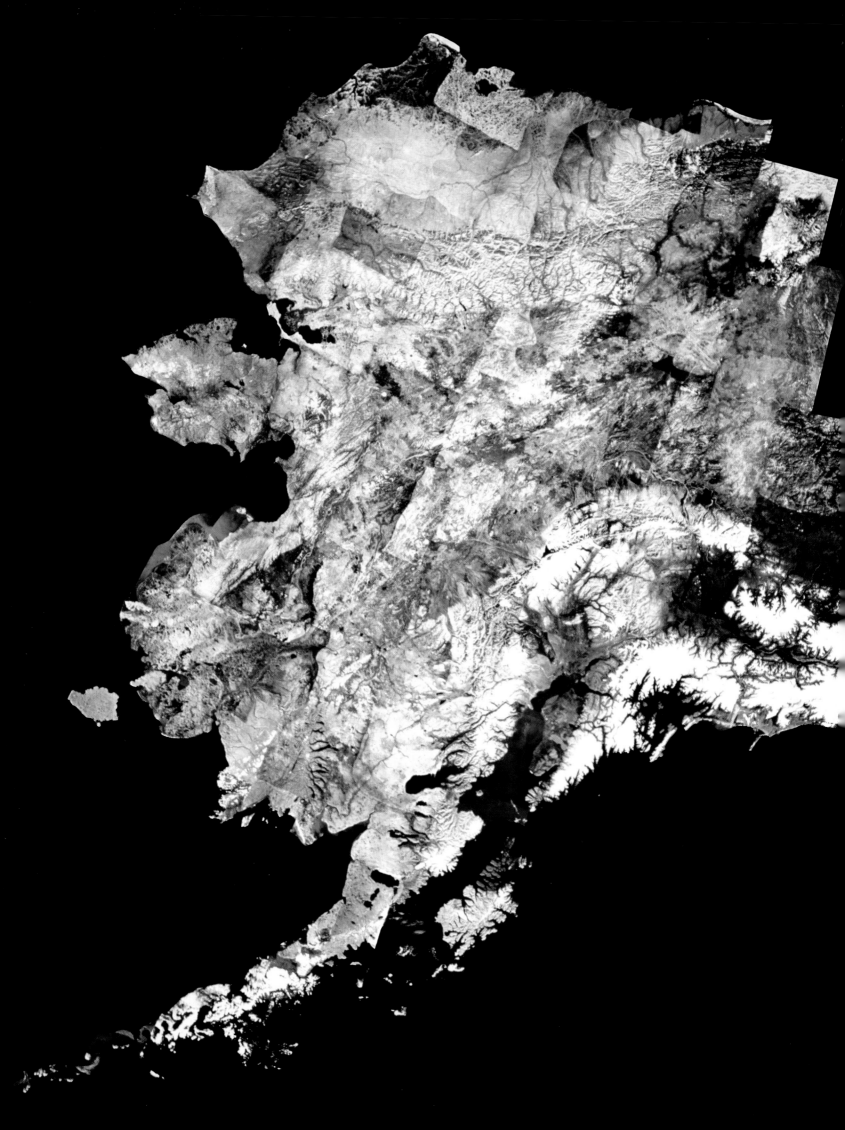

ALASKA – THE GREAT LAND by Lowell Thomas, Jr.

A thousand and more years ago, the people known as Aleut, who lived among the stormy string of Aleutian Islands that reaches across the north Pacific Ocean from the American continent almost to Asia looked to the northeast to see the mainland. »Alyeska,« they called it, the place where the waves begin. As the white man came into the land of the Aleuts and learned the word, the place where the waves begin became the great land and that's the definition that has persevered – The Great Land. And, great it was, and is today – Alaska, the 49th star in the U.S. flag and America's last frontier. But this vast new state faces great challenge in the decade of the 1980s and beyond, because it has both promise and problems in abundance. And the way Alaska fulfills its promise and meets its problems will have a critical impact not only on its own future but upon the rest of the United States and the rest of the world as well.

A wealth of precious resources lies within its boundaries: nonrenewable and renewable resources, wildlife and wilderness unmatched anywhere in the world. The statistics are truly staggering. Alaska has 80 percent of the shoreline of the United States. It contains 375 million acres which span 21 degrees of latitude, 43 degrees of longitude, and encompasses four time zones stretching across 2,400 miles. Within its borders are three million lakes of 40 or more acres; 10.9 million acres of glaciers and ice fields; 10,000 streams and rivers totalling more than 365,000 miles in length. And there are seven mountain ranges with 19 peaks topping 14,000 feet, including 20,320 foot Mt. McKinley, the tallest mountain on the North American continent.

Alaska is a land that inspires superlatives. »Beautiful, magnificent, awe-inspiring, gigantic« are all adjectives that describe it correctly, but they all fall woefully flat in attempting to describe its essence. From the air, parts of the state appear as vast fields of mountain peaks running away to the horizon, while elsewhere the appearance is that of a green-colored ocean of seemingly endless forests and tundra. The beauty and diversity are breathtaking.

This is, indeed, a great land. Its 586,000 square miles comprise an area equal to one-fifth of the total land area of the other 49 states. When a map of Alaska is superimposed on an identical scale map of Europe, from east to west it covers the area from just south of Kiev in the Soviet Union, to Manchester, England, and north to south, from Oslo, Norway, into Morocco in Africa.

Beyond its enormous physical size, the statistics of Alaska's resources are equally impressive. Estimates of recoverable oil reserves range from 12 to 94 billion barrels. The state's official guess is 75 billion barrels, a figure equal to one-fourth of the estimated total United States undiscovered reserves onshore and two-thirds of the nation's undiscovered offshore oil. Alaska is thought to contain 380 trillion cubic feet of natural gas – one-tenth of the nation's onshore reserves. Coal reserves are estimated at 24 billion (!) tons of bituminous and 558 billion (!) tons of subbituminous coal. And the state is known to be a storehouse of minerals, including a number of strategic ones which are presently being imported from other nations.

In addition to nonrenewable resources, Alaska is blessed with an abundance of those that regenerate themselves. Its fisheries are among the most productive in the world and it has rich stores of timber, almost unlimited hydroelectric potential; agriculture, too, holds some promise.

The Great Land also has a wealth of scenery and wildlife. About 20 percent of the entire North American waterfowl population breeds within its borders – some 12 million ducks, 1 million geese, 70,000 swans and 150,000 cranes. It also is a habitat for several endangered species such as the Aleutian Canada goose and American and Arctic peregrine falcon. Although bald eagles are endangered in many parts of the United States, they thrive in Alaska. Many terrestrial mammals live here, too; small fur bearers such as beaver, lynx and fox, as well as larger animals: moose, sheep, goats, wolves, musk oxen and three species of bears. Herds of caribou make their home on the tundra, feeding on lichen. Twenty-seven species of marine mammals, including whales, live along Alaska's coastline. Sea life exists in great variety in marine waters, while lakes and streams support many fish, including five kinds of salmon, steelhead and rainbow trout, lake trout, grayling, arctic char and whitefish.

Those who are unfamiliar with Alaska often think of it as an enormous homogeneous mass of ice and snow populated by a few Eskimos living in igloos. The reality is that this state has a vast diversity of terrain, climate and wildlife, along with a diversity of people and cultures – and no igloos! Actually, there is not one Alaska, but at least six, ranging from the rain forests of the Southeast to the Arctic tundra of the north. And the maritime coast along the Gulf of Alaska differs greatly from the dry interior, while the Aleutian Islands have a stormy character quite distinct from that of the Bering Sea Coast. At the southern tip of the Panhandle in Southeastern it seldom snows, while far to the north along the Arctic Coast, it may snow even in mid-summer. Even so, the Arctic Coast is considered a desert as in many years it receives less than five inches of precipitation. Scattered across this varied land are approximately 420,000 people, comparable to the population of Albuquerque, New Mexico. About half of them live in Anchorage, while the rest are found in a handful of other major communities or in the many remote and widely separated villages of 100 or fewer persons.

Who are these people? Except for the native people – the Eskimos, Aleuts and Indians who comprise about 16 percent of the state's population – nearly everyone came from somewhere else; it is relatively rare to find a non-Native who was born and raised in Alaska.

At one time most Alaska immigrants were just plain fortune seekers, while others sought a chance for a new start of one sort or another. Later on, though, more headed north in answer to the »call of the wild,« eager to live in a land of great scenic beauty, an unspoiled wilderness where a person has greater freedom to live in his own style without feeling crowded. In recent times an increasing percentage of newcomers fall into this last category, and although many come following the promise of riches, fewer now are the »get-rich-quick« type. But, there is no way to pigeon-hole any of them. On the one hand, Alaska has its »go-for-broke« land developers and used-car salesmen, while at the other extreme are the bush pilots who thrive on dangerous missions into the Alaska bush and the brawny fur trappers who spend the long winters alone with their dog teams on the trap line or with their snowmobiles. The one thing they all have in common, those who choose to stay, is a love of the land – and a fierce independence tempered by a ready willingness to help one another in time of need.

Another fairly common characteristic, especially among those who have lived here for a dozen or more years, is a distrust of the U.S. government and major corporations. Their distrust is based on a long history of exploitation during territorial days, extending into early statehood. For most of its past, Alaska has been treated like a colony – a place to extract gold, copper, fur, fish and timber – always taking and leaving nothing behind but »holes in the ground« as a senior legislator used to say. Russian fur traders prior to 1867 were even worse, decimating the sea otter population and nearly annihilating the Aleuts through forced servitude.

Native Alaskans, too, have been wary of outsiders. And they also vary greatly in culture and lifestyle, speaking 22 separate and distinct languages. There is no typical Alaska Native any more than there is a single Alaska. Some still live in the traditional lifestyles, although no one is completely untouched

mobiles as much a way of life for villagers as dog sleds. Although the state has instituted a bilingual education program and has built schools in many villages so youngsters don't have to leave their

homes to obtain an education, some of the traditional ways are being lost. Many young Eskimos and Indians move to Anchorage which now has a larger Native population than any other community in the state, or to Fairbanks or the few other larger population centers.

While Alaska's non-Native population has grown enormously since the influx of gold seekers late in the 19th century, the Native population has remained relatively stable. The number of persons enrolled under the Alaska Native Claims Settlement Act of 1971 was about 68,000, including those who now live outside of the state.

The settlement of the Native claims, pushed through Congress primarily to secure clear right-of-way for construction of the Trans-Alaska oil pipeline, has had a tremendous effect over the past decade. It allocated 44 million acres of land and nearly $1 billion to 13 regional Native corporations and more than 100 village corporations. The regional corporations have invested in numerous business ventures with varying success. For instance, Native corporations own two of the major hotels in Anchorage, including the Calista Corporation's plush new Sheraton Anchorage. NANA Corporation has been one of the more successful and has undertaken a number of enterprises, including providing security services during pipeline construction. NANA also has a reindeer herd among its commercial endeavors.

While the claims act has markedly benefited the Native population, it has not been a cure-all. Many villagers live in poverty, and alcoholism is a tragic problem. Native people have, however, fared better than most Indian tribes in the Lower 48 states. They have been able to maintain their traditional ways of life and never were placed on reservations. The U.S. Department of Interior at one time did attempt to institute a reservation system for Alaska's Natives, but it was opposed so widely that the idea was dropped.

Throughout Alaska's history – beginning with the enslavement of the Aleuts by Russian fur traders in the 1790's – there have been clashes between the original inhabitants and those who came to Alaska from other nations. The latest clash has been over high seas whaling, a stringent quota imposed by the International Whaling Commission upon the Eskimos who have subsisted in part upon bowhead whales for centuries. It has been hard for these skin-boat whalers to understand why their traditional way of life should be curtailed, and difficult to explain their needs to the Commission.

With the many different cultures and traditions represented in Alaska, and the tremendous diversity of the land and its peoples, it is not surprising that there has been conflict over the use of resources and the future of the state. One prime example has been a ten-year battle over so-called »Alaska national interest lands.« The 1971 claims settlement act contained a section which called for designation of up to 80 million acres within the new state as national parks and other conservation units. That provision gave Congress eight years to act on the withdrawals. But when the time ran out with no Congressional action, the President and the Secretary of Interior moved to protect nearly 100 million acres from development pending a legislative solution. Congress, then, did agree finally in November 1980 on a bill that set aside more than 100 million acres of Alaska as wilderness, national parks, wildlife refuges, wild and scenic rivers, and the like.

A coalition of national environmentalist organizations had been pushing for more restrictive legislation, contending it was needed to protect the last unspoiled wilderness left, while the state held that the legislation was too restrictive, unnecessarily setting aside vast chunks of land without allowing for even the most careful development of the resources it contained.

Apart from the merits of the specific measure passed by Congress, settlement of the land issue cleared up uncertainty that had clouded the future. Most important, it fulfilled a promise of the Alaska Statehood Act of 1959 that the new state could select 104 million acres from the U.S. government (about 28 percent of the total land area) for its entitlement, on which to build a viable economy. Until 1980, and because of a long-standing »freeze« imposed by the federal government upon Alaska's lands, the state had firm title to only 21 million acres with tentative approval of another 15 million acres. One of the provisions of the bill passed by Congress was the lifting of that »freeze« and the conveyance of state and Native land selections.

Along with its tremendous potential, Alaska has some special problems. To begin with, the cost of living is much higher than the national average. Food costs in Anchorage are about 35 percent greater, while in other communities they are even higher. In Barrow, for example, on the shore of the Arctic Ocean, food costs are about 250 percent of the national average. And the cost of electricity and fuel in rural areas is staggering, forcing more and more rural residents who have traditionally relied on a subsistence economy to seek cash-paying jobs.

Unemployment, too, is chronically high, particularly in rural areas. And the overall economy has been sluggish since completion of the Trans-Alaska oil pipeline in 1977. Bankruptcies have soared, while the number of building permits has dropped considerably.

Inasmuch as delays have plagued the startup of construction of a proposed national gas pipeline to carry North Slope gas to the Lower states, there have been no major construction projects to fill the void left in the economy by completion of the oil line.

In addition to high prices and a sluggish economy, Alaska has been plagued by high crime rates, high divorce and suicide rates and other social problems. And the consumption of alcohol per capita is the highest in the nation. For instance, in September, 1980, Alaskans bought more than one million gallons of alcoholic beverages – an average of close to five gallons per adult – in one month alone!

Looking to the future, one of the biggest decisions will be the use of Alaska's enormous, though temporary, oil wealth. When the Trans-Alaska pipeline went onstream, Alaska began receiving in royalties 12.5 percent of the value of the oil produced, and this together with severance and other related taxes will earn the state billions of dollars. For example, in 1983, the state's petroleum revenues are expected to be about $3 billion. Future revenues, however, will depend on the development of world oil prices.

How best to use this tremendous wealth will be a subject of major debate throughout the decade. Rumors of a bonanza of oil money have spread across the United States, with unfounded talk of the state »giving away« untold fortunes. The truth is far less dramatic. The 1980 legislature repealed the state income tax, which was among the nation's highest. The legislature as well passed a dividend program to come from a permanent fund of oil revenues which would have paid every resident $50 for each full year of residence since statehood in 1959. The dividend program was successfully challenged in court but the permanent fund remained while the legislature wrestled with the problem of how to distribute some of the state's oil wealth to residents. In 1982, each resident was paid $1,000 from the proceeds of that fund.

Once before, in 1969, Alaska had an oil bonanza from lease sales and $900 million was consumed during the next decade, primarily through increases in government. The people of Alaska learned a lesson from that and now have voted for a type of savings plan to set aside some of the oil money for the time when nonrenewable resources are exhausted. They have approved a constitutional amendment creating the permanent investment fund into which shall be placed at least 25 percent of all bonus bid income and royalties on oil and gas leases and stipulating that those monies may not be spent for government operations. The permanent fund's principal, then, may only be invested – and in such safe securities as U.S. government bonds.

By 1982, more than $3.5 billion had been funneled into this permanent fund. A primary focus in the use of the fund's earnings will be the development of renewable resource industries within the state. Alaska's permanent fund removes the temptation to squander the entire oil windfall through ever-expanding public programs and a general growth in government. The increase in the state budget from less than $100 million before the North Slope lease sales of 1969 to $4.4 billion for fiscal year 1982 shows the need to set aside at least part of the oil revenue bonanza.

Exaggerated stories regarding Alaska's wealth even sparked talk in Congress about sharing the wealth through some form of taxation on the state's oil revenues. Aside from setting a dangerous precedent in the free enterprise system, the scheme ignored the catching up that Alaska has to do in providing even basic services to its people. For instance, despite the vastness of the land, there are only 10,000 miles of public roads, only about half of them paved. And transportation systems, both in rural and urban areas, are inadequate. Then, too, many rural villages do not have adequate water or sewer systems, and telephone service is a relatively new phenomenon in some areas and those villages that do have a phone usually have but one. The state initiated a program several years ago to bring both telephone service and satellite television to every rural village – one example of an innovative, costly program that would not be necessary in other states. The temporary oil bonanza will nowhere fully meet the people's legitimate needs.

Despite the rhetoric of extreme environmentalists who painted us as »rape, ruin and run boys« during the Congressional debate on the lands legislation, most Alaskans are concerned about protecting the environment and scenic wonders that drew them to the northern frontier in the first place. Today's pioneer cares for the land as never before. He has seen, tasted and smelled the pollution plaguing many parts of the United States – and other parts of the world – and wants no more of it. He is glad to see large sections of the state set aside as parks, wildlife preserves and national forests; and he believes development based upon oil and gas, timber and other resources, must be pursued with far greater sensitivity to nature than elsewhere in earlier times. To this end, he has supported state air and water pollution laws which are national models, and oil tanker ship safety laws that are the nation's toughest. Evidence of this attitude surfaced dramatically in 1974 when Jay Hammond and I ran as a team for governor and lieutenant governor and were elected on a simple platform:
1. Respect for the environment and strict observance of environmental safeguards;
2. Orderly, well planned development;
3. Maximum public participation in decision making.

While those who favored development at any cost decried us as »no-growthers« who would kill the economy, a majority of Alaskans agreed with us that development should be balanced against the benefit to the state and the cost to the environment. And they re-elected Governor Hammond for a second (and last) term in 1978. Alaska's environmental record has been generally good. From the small amount of land actually transferred to the state prior to 1980, we have created the largest state park system in the nation. And three of the parks are larger than those of any other states: Wood-Tikchik, Denali, and Chugach State Parks.

Even though neither side was satisfied completely with the Alaska lands bill finally enacted by Congress, its passage marked Alaska's coming of age after more than 20 years as a state. Now is has the means to develop a stable, diversified economy. A most hopeful sign for the future is the permanent fund, to the degree that its income is used to promote renewable resource industries.

Also, increases in tourism bode well for the future, for tourism is Alaska's second or third biggest industry (oil development and commercial fishing being the others), depending on the manner in which the economic indicators are calculated. Some day it probably will rank Number 1. The number of pleasure visitors in 1982 reached a record 690,000 and that figure is expected to reach 1 million by 1986. Efforts are being made to promote tourism as a year-around industry, with ski tours as one major attraction.

Fishing is another area of continued promise. A potential for a new bottomfish industry exists now that the 200 mile offshore limit is in effect. A federal Commerce Department study indicates the bottomfish industry could generate $258 million a year in wages and profits within 10 years, creating 14,000 new jobs. At present, the bottomfish industry is dominated by Japan, the Soviet Union and South Korea. Even so, commercial fish landings in Alaska in 1980 totaled about 1 billion pounds, valued at $560 million, mostly from salmon, halibut and king crab.

Timber, mining and agriculture are other major growth industries and international trade is becoming increasingly important. In 1981, Alaska exported $1,182,597,000 worth of goods to other nations, the bulk of it to Japan. That was an increase of almost $200 million from the previous year. Alaska exports forests products, seafood, natural gas, urea and ammonia. And coal from the Usibelli mine may be next under a contract to be signed with a Korean company in 1983. Oil, because of a condition in pipeline legislation, is not exported.

Alaska is becoming increasingly aware of the potential for international trade. For several years it has maintained an office in Tokyo. Foreign nations are investing heavily in Alaska, although exact figures are not available. Japanese firms have invested in the wood products and fisheries industries; the government of France has made investments in wholesale petroleum products, and the volume of international air travel is on the rise as upwards of a dozen foreign-based carriers touch down at Anchorage on their way between Europe and the Orient.

Alaska, »The Great Land,« is maturing rapidly in its relationships with other states and other nations, and the future looks bright, indeed, for continued growth during the 1980s and beyond. With a careful balance between resource development and protection of its physical beauty, Alaska can be both an energy storehouse for future generations, and an inspiring, soul-satisfying natural wonderland for people from the far corners of the earth.

Alaska Marine Highway's state ferries provide regular transportation throughout the Southeast and between the Kenai Peninsula and Valdez and Cordova, as well as Kodiak Island. Scenic fjords such as the Lynn Canal add to the pleasure of traveling.

The Alaska Railroad, the world's most northern, operates on 470 miles of mainline track between Fairbanks, Anchorage and the Kenai Peninsula; on its way to Anchorage it runs through a scenic wonderland alongside the Turnagain Arm with the Kenai Peninsula's northcoast mountains in the background.

Riverboat *Discovery II* on the Chena River, near Fairbanks; today a tourist attraction, her predecessors provided transportation and pleasure cruises on the Tanana and Yukon Rivers, upstream as far as Dawson City.

Anchorage, with close to 200,000 people the biggest and fastest growing city in Alaska and located on the upper shores of Cook Inlet, has a moderate »Great Lakes« climate. It's a city of contrasts, where fancy hotels and skyscraper restaurants overlook salmon-spawning streams and where flocks of wild birds nest in Lake Hood (and Lake Spenard), largest floatplane home base in the world, adjacent to Anchorage International Airport.

Mt. McKinley, called by Native Indians »Denali« – the big one –, at 20,320 feet North America's highest mountain, is the focal point for Denali National Park and Preserve (formerly Mt. McKinley National Park); this parkland is Alaska's best known wilderness recreation area.   ▷

An hour's drive north of Anchorage lies the Matanuska Valley, Alaska's »breadbasket;« long hours of daylight during the growing season produce wheelbarrow-sized cabbages and »Alaskan-sized« vegetables. Farms nestle beneath craggy mountain peaks and glaciers, such as the Knik Glacier.

Oil rigs at Kemik, 80 miles south of Prudhoe Bay, in the crackling cold of early spring's sun.

The largest coal operation in the state is the Usibelli strip mine at Healy, just north of the Alaska Range.

Fish packer and seiners in stormy Southeastern Alaska waters.

Family fishing: seining pink salmon.

Commercial king crab fishing near Kodiak Island.

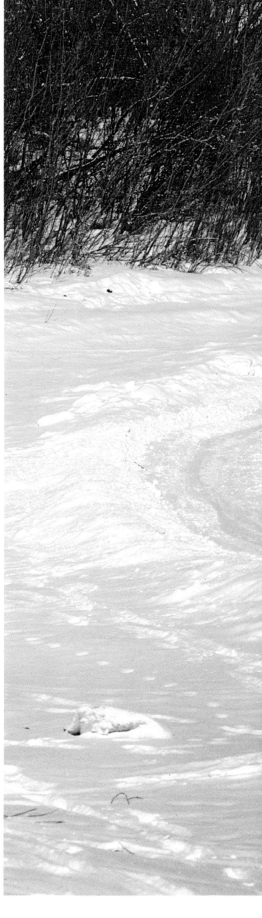

Start of the famed
Iditarod Trail Sled
Dog Race at
Anchorage in early
March of each year.
The race attracts
visitors from all over

the state and from
many other parts of
the world. Man and
animal have to give
their very best in
strength and spirit.

Dog mushing:
Alaskan traditional
sled dog race.

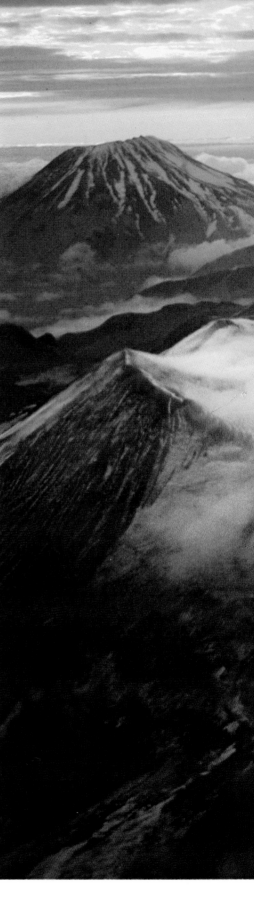

The Aleutian Islands and the Alaska Peninsula are part of the »rim of fire« that surrounds the Pacific Basin. Mt. Katmai, one of the region's many active volcanoes, produced a major eruption, when in 1912 pumice and ash was spewed through its Novarupta outlet over 3,000 sq.miles of southwest Alaska; the Valley of Ten Thousand Smokes was one result of it. The eruption of Akutan Volcano in 1978 shows that this whole area will not remain quiet, as is also proven by frequent earthquakes in this and other south-central Alaskan regions.

Over a century ago Sitka was the capital of Russian-America; many examples of ecclesiastical art and icons from those days are exhibited in the

Cathedral of St. Michael, an Orthodox church in downtown Sitka. Located at the western shores of Baranof Island and nestled in typical

Southeastern fjord landscape, Sitka's harbor is home for hundreds of commercial fishing boats and pleasure cruisers.

Tenakee Springs, a small resort village located on the shores of an inlet of Chichagof Island and serviced regularly by state ferries.

Juneau, Alaska's state capital with 21,000 inhabitants, crouches at the base of Mt. Juneau, facing Gastineau Channel and Douglas Island.

Of all Southeastern cities, Juneau offers the longest stretch of paved roads, giving access to numerous glaciers and whitewater rivers.

Alaska's southernmost city, Ketchikan, is one of the largest of the Panhandle and a busy port for commercial fishing boats; timber

is another important industry. Ketchikan is, as well, the starting-point for sightseeing flights and yacht tours to the Misty Fjords National Monument.

Overlooking Glacier Bay's Muir Inlet, this national park is one of Southeastern Alaska's most dramatic attractions. Part of the

Fairweather Range of the St. Elias Mountains, it encloses 16 active tidewater glaciers and the huge Brady Icefield.

Bald eagles thrive in many parts of Alaska; one of the largest populations in the world can be found at the Chilkat River in the Southeast, near

the Indian village of Klukwan.

Horned puffins chatter and flutter on the rocky ledge of one of the Pribilof Islands, a tiny windswept archipelago in the

Bering Sea; large populations of puffins are found in many other coastal areas of Alaska as well.

THE SETTLERS by Larry Beck

The history of the white settlement of Alaska could be one of dates and places and political events and wars, but if one gets right down to it, the history of any place is the story of its people. As Alaska began to grow, many accepted the challenges of the North and many perished. Many, too, took to the Great Land and its harsh climate, thriving and building as they went. The true history of Alaska is told in the lives of those people whose pioneer spirit led them to accept greater and greater challenges, following legends and creating legends as they went. Their legends are the heritage of Alaska.

RIDING THE CIRCUIT

The judge sits in solitary dignity in long black robes. The courtroom is paneled in oak or walnut. The temperature is comfortable. The crowd is respectful. Work in one of many federal courtrooms in Alaska goes on today. But times were different when the gold rush was on and one man rode the circuit of the Third Judicial District. His courtroom was of log if he was lucky. Sometimes he settled disputes in the middle of the street. Sometimes a saloon became his courtroom. But wherever he went, his presence was felt and Alaska was better for it. The judge was James Wickersham.

Wickersham was the oldest in a large family from southern Illinois. He remembered watching his uncle march off to serve in the Civil War. And for many years, a proud possession was a small American flag presented to him by a weary veteran. Following his law studies at the hands of former Governor John McAuley Palmer, Wickersham and his wife and son moved west. He ended up in Tacoma, Washington, where he spent years in law practice and politics. He was also an avid outdoorsman who enjoyed hiking in the rugged wilderness. He was one of the first to suggest that part of that rugged beauty of Washington's Olympic Range be placed into a national park.

The judgeships in Alaska were not often granted on merit. More often, they were given to political cronies of powerful senators or businessmen in Washington who either had to repay a favor or wished to employ the help of a not-so-honest judge in acquiring some mining interests in Alaska. Wickersham was a political appointment, but he proved to be well above the average.

He was also above the average age of the people traveling to Alaska at the turn of the century. He was 43. His wife was 37. Not the young couple starting out in life, certainly, since one son was at the Naval Academy at Annapolis already. He was given the least promising and least popular district – Eagle. This included 300,000 square miles with fewer than 1,500 white inhabitants. The town of Eagle City was a bustling trading center for miners, but there were certainly few of the trappings of civilization. No school. No courthouse. No jail.

Wickersham was authorized to reserve two town lots for a courthouse and jail and to have them constructed as long as the cost didn't exceed $5,000. But there was a catch. The $5,000 had to be raised from license fees levied and collected on the saloon owners and merchants in town. The day after his arrival, Wickersham began levying fees. But even after collecting the necessary money, he had to fight the ever-present red tape of government bureaucracy in order to get permission to use the military sawmill to process his lumber. He finally received permission and the building was erected.

Another tussle with bureaucracy over a bottle of »subsistence« was not so successful. Before the river iced over, Wickersham wanted to travel down the Yukon to Circle and Rampart. Naturally, he planned to hold court, but he also needed to levy those necessary fees to pay for his courthouse. Just opposite Coal Creek, their boat, the *Suzie,* ran aground on a sandbar where it remained stranded for two days. The judge and his court officials transferred to a smaller boat and continued on to Circle. They left several old men behind who had been picked for jury duty. Wickersham felt he should provide some food for these men since no one really knew how long it would be before the *Suzie* floated free. Along with the food, Wickersham authorized a bottle of whiskey to »help keep them warm.«

When later making up the official report, the deputy marshall came to Wickersham asking how to list the bottle of whiskey. The judge replied that it should be charged up as subsistence, the same as the food. The deputy was precise. He listed: »one basket of food, $10; one bottle of subsistence, $5.« For more than two years, correspondence concerning that bottle traveled between Washington and Alaska. The marshall's office never did get paid that $5.

In order to cover his circuit that first winter, Wickersham had to travel by dog team and snowshoe. It was a 1,140 mile round trip from Eagle to Circle and Rampart and took 45 days.

Wickersham traveled with his clerk and other court officials as well as a deputy marshall and often the mail carrier. He used a five dog team loaded with 300 pounds on his Indian made spruce sled. The load included dog food, rice, bacon, dried fish, blankets, dry socks and warm clothing, extra harnesses and caribou skin »booties« for the dog's trail-sore feet.

Many who have seen the movie version of a musher balanced on the runners of a sled as it moves smoothly over packed snow have no idea of the realities of traveling in interior Alaska at the turn of the century. Periods spent riding the runners were few. Most of the time, Wickersham was either slogging along behind the sled or breaking trail for his dogs as winds piled the snow into hard, solid drifts.

On January 21, Wickersham wrote in his diary »I walked ahead of the team all day long with the wind in my face breaking trail. The constant rolling all day pretty nearly lamed me in the ankles and I can hardly walk tonight.« Another day he wrote, »As we came down the bank of the Seventy Mile River, I held back on the handle bars, the sled upset, caught me and turned my heels where my head was, and threw me several feet out into the snowbank. Forty degrees below.«

Blisters developed as a result of his favoring the sore ankle. The only remedy on the trail was to open the blisters and pour on coal oil from the lantern. He developed snowblindness and stated, »My eyes feel as if they are filled with sand and I keep them covered with a bandage and hold on to the handle bars of the sled for guidance.« He was lucky. He had companions and good trail dogs who could help him along the way. He was also lucky in the fact that he had always been an outdoorsman and was in what he had considered fairly good shape.

During his 45-days trip, Wickersham levied fees and dispensed justice with a firm and steady hand. His reputation would grow in the coming years.

James Wickersham was not always popular, however, with those in power. His refusal to allow powerful men to run roughshod over the miners and their claims resulted in the fact that his appointment to a second term was resisted in the Senate. The President solved the problem with »recess appointments« given to Wickersham while the Senate was in recess.

His wife wanted him to quit. They had lost a son to the cruel winters. Her health was not good. But Wickersham had found his place. For more than 39 years he was a strong spirit in Alaska and his credits are remarkable: Delegate to Congress, first to attempt to climb Mt. McKinley, first to introduce a statehood bill, and guiding light behind the founding of the University of Alaska. As he traveled, he recorded all the judicial decisions that had been made in the territory since it was acquired from Russia in 1867. He also was the first to advocate a Native land claims settlement and convinced the federal government that a railroad was a necessity in Alaska.

There are men in Alaska's history who may be better known to the world at large. But no man stands taller in his drive to achieve the best for his adopted land than the man who started out riding the circuit of District Number 3 in Alaska.

E. A. HEGG

Photographing Alaska's rugged grandeur is fairly easy these days. Lenses of all types make it easy to focus on the tiniest of tundra flowers or the most majestic of mountain peaks. Film speeds allow us to take photos in almost any light. And where the light is not adequate, a wide range of flash attachments is available to fill in the necessary light. Instant films and cameras make us able to view our work immediately and shoot another photo if we are not completely satisfied.

All of these modern conveniences were certainly not available to E.A. Hegg, and yet his photos stand as a record of the history of Alaska and the Yukon in a time when the spirit of the north was at its height. Many people have seen his work without knowing who took those crisp black and white scenes of men and women forming a winding chain over the Chilkoot Pass. Or they may have seen a street scene of Skagway or Dawson at the height of the gold rush. Teeming streets and interesting people were favorite subjects of Hegg.

Little is known of Hegg the man. But thousands of photos tell us what kind of a photographer he was. We know he was born in Sweden, migrated to Wisconsin and ended up in the Pacific Northwest. It was there that he opened a studio at the young age of 15. In addition to the standard photos of young brides and grooms, young children, families and businessmen, Hegg wandered the forests of the area shooting scenes of men at work in the logging industry.

He answered the call of the gold fields and traveled north in time to record the arrival of thousands on the beaches of Skagway and Dyea. With bulky camera on his back he traveled the passes himself, recording the frantic rush to the fields. He set up shop in tents along the way, providing photos to homesick stampeders eager to send home some memento.

These exciting scenes of the world's greatest gold rush are all the more remarkable when you realize that they were taken with a bulky camera and primitive lenses. Rather than the coated film of today, Hegg had to create his own albumen formula from eggs and apply it to glass plates. If the light was not bright enough, he simply could not take a photograph.

Hegg and his camera captured the descent from the steep mountain passes down to the Yukon headwater lakes in Canada and the feverish boat building on the shores. He caught the stampeders as they launched these flimsy craft and fought the all-water route to Dawson via the treacherous Whitehorse Rapids and Miles Canyon.

He recorded the work in the placer gold fields – above ground when the muck was brought up and run through the sluice boxes and below ground where miners had only candles available for long-time-exposures.

When gold was discovered in Nome, Hegg journeyed there. His unerring eye and lens captured the tent city, the men and women working in the Ruby Sands with the famous »long tom« version of the sluice box. As the city grew into something more permanent, Hegg again built a studio. He recorded the early romance of Nome with its dog sledding, disastrous fires and floods, and its places of pleasure.

Everywhere he went, Hegg advertised. Many of his photos of Skagway include his well known sign. Others along the trail show his banner reading »Views of Alaska and the Klondike.« His little boat which served as a field darkroom carried the same caption.

Once, Hegg got together a team of goats to pull his sled. Advertising was naturally added to the sides of the sled. The goats were great at pulling. And, after a summer of being fattened on the grasses of the region, they became a winter treat for sourdoughs eating a diet of mainly beans and dried foods.

Hegg became the official photographer for the Guggenheim/Morgan syndicate and recorded the building of »The Iron Trail,« the famous Copper River and Northwestern Railroad out of Cordova. Here again, he built a studio and recorded not only the feverish railroad construction, but the growing fishing and canning industry in that coastal area.

Hegg had the same wanderlust as those he photographed. He moved from town to town around Alaska before finally retiring in California. He probably didn't even feel that his work was that important. Many of his glass slides were found years later when a cabin was torn down and the walls revealed the slides.

His scrapbooks, now recognized as priceless records of an era, were rescued from the city dump in Seattle. Now most of his work is well preserved in the University of Washington Library.

Hegg was one who was a success in the gold rush without ever having searched for gold. His wanderlust was satisfied as he traveled across Alaska and the Yukon as the rushes began and petered out. In his lifetime he simply did not realize what his tireless wanderings had produced. This one man had captured an era on glass – the opening up of the great state that is now Alaska.

THE SERUM RACE TO NOME

Nome was isolated during the winter of 1925. Airplanes had made their debut in Alaska, but the open cockpits made winter flying impossible. The last ships had made their runs north with supplies.

There was a telegraph system run by the Army Signal Corps. And dog teams provided mail delivery and supplied some commercial goods. But there was no road to Nome. No railroad.

Dr. Curtis Welch had been called to examine two sick children. These children, ages three and one, had shallow breathing and light rapid pulse. Their mother said they'd been sick for three days with what she had thought was a cold. Their throats were extremely sore and the doctor couldn't get them to open their mouths. Despite all his efforts, the children died the next day.

A few days later, he was summoned to the home of Richard Stanley. This time, Dr. Welch could get Richard to open his mouth and the sight of the dirty white patches of the diphtheria membrane shocked, saddened and frightened him. Dr. Welch had only 80,000 units of antitoxin, and that was 5 years old. The prescribed dosage was 10,000 units. He remembered the flu epidemic of 1919 and knew that unless the disease was checked immediately, the entire town could be threatened. The Eskimos had no resistance at all to the white man's diseases and there were 91 »flu orphans« alone, while whole villages also had been wiped out.

Welch had requested new antitoxin that summer, but the Seattle office of the Public Health Service had not responded. Now it was too late.

Dr. Welch went to Mayor George Maynard who called an emergency meeting of the city council. They knew that they would not only have to act to enforce the quarantine set up by Dr. Welch, but they had to get antitoxin to Nome – quickly.

Thought was given to trying an airplane, but the idea was quickly abandoned. The men turned to the route that they knew could be the most reliable – rail to Nenana and then dog team relay to Nome. They planned to have one of Nome's own mushers meet the relay team halfway, at about Nulato.

Dr. Welch sent a priority message to Juneau, Fairbanks and Seward telling everyone of Nome's desperate need.

One million, one hundred units of serum were located in Seattle and plans were made immediately to ship the antitoxin north. But widespread relief was felt when it was discovered that 300,000 units were already in Alaska at the Alaska Railroad Hospital in Anchorage. While this wasn't enough, the amount could help to stem the tide until the other serum arrived.

Governor Scott Bone contacted the Northern Commercial Company which had trading posts, stores and riverboats in Alaska's interior. They also had the U.S. Mail contract. Mail drivers were quickly recruited via the »mukluk telegraph,« that mysterious method by which news travels throughout the north.

The serum was packed in cylinders, wrapped in quilting and on January 26, it was delivered to the Alaska Railroad for shipment to Nenana. Two hundred ninety-eight miles away, the first musher was waiting. That same day, Leonhard Seppala was sent out from Nome to race toward Nulato. The people of Nome did not yet know that a most effective relay had already been formed and the serum would be brought almost to Nome before Seppala had to take over.

»Wild Bill« Shannon was the first. The temperature dropped to −50°F as he ran. He had to slow his team so they wouldn't freeze their lungs. At Tolovana, Shannon met his friend, Dan Green. As they warmed the serum for 45 minutes, Dan told Bill the bad news – 15 more diphtheria cases in Nome and 4 more deaths. This knowledge made the relay all the more important to Green as he set out in −30° temperatures with 20 knot winds.

The serum was passed along from musher to musher: Dan Green to Johnny Folger to Sam Joseph who ran his designated 26 miles in 2 hours and 40 minutes. Titus Nickoli followed, running 34 miles to Kallands where he handed the precious bundle to Dave Corning. Dave was followed by Edgar Kalland and then Harry Pitka.

At Ruby, Pitka turned the serum over to Billy McCarty. Ruby was famous for its dogs and the Ruby Derby. Billy had picked out seven of the best dogs, and he headed them toward Whiskey Creek. He encountered a snow storm, but drove on in very poor visibility.

Edgar Nollner met him at Whiskey Creek with his champion team and famous lead dog, Dixie. He counted on her to set a fast pace, and she did. His older brother George took over at Galena.

Charlie Evans had one of the toughest legs. It was 30 miles from Bishop Mountain to Nulato. Ten miles along the trail he ran into open water where the Koyukuk River ran into the Yukon. Besides having to carefully skirt the open water, he had to travel in the ice fog formed by the open water. When he arrived at Koyukuk, his father urged him to rest, but Charlie was afraid he couldn't get his dogs started again so he pressed on.

Tommy Patsey ran 36 miles from Nulato to Kaltag, averaging a little better than 10 miles per hour. Other mushers took over: »Jackscrew,« Victor Anagick, Myles Gonangnan who had to travel through another storm and white-outs where the horizon simply disappears.

At Shaktoolik, Gonangnan turned the serum over to Henry Ivanoff. A half mile out of town he ran into trouble. His team caught the scent of a reindeer and tried to pursue it. He braked, and halted the team, but in their frustration the dogs began fighting. While he was trying to straighten out the mess of angry, fight-

ing fur, he saw another team heading north toward him. It was Leonhard Seppala.

People could recognize Seppala's team instantly. It was made up of Siberian huskies, often called »Plume-tailed rats« because of their size. Seppala was halted and the serum transferred to his sled and the race home began.

In trying to decide whether to skirt Norton Bay or take the short route to Isaac's Point, Seppala said he thought of the suffering in his home and headed out over the short cut, braving the danger of open channels forming in the ice.

He thought he would have to run the entire distance back to Nome. He didn't know that, after his departure, other mushers were sent along the route to wait for him and bring the serum back. After traveling through blizzards for 84 miles without a rest, the team reached the north side of Norton Bay. They stopped at an Eskimo's sod igloo where the dogs received a ration of salmon and blubber and the serum was warmed. Early the next morning they started off again. When he finally reached Golovin, his dogs dropped in their tracks in front of Dexter's Roadhouse. There were 78 miles to go to Nome.

Charles Olson took over and ran 25 miles of the roughest trail yet in −30°F temperatures with 40 knot winds. At one point, the winds swept Olson and his team into a tangle. The dogs were freezing and Olson received frost bite from taking off his gloves to wrap blankets around the dogs.

When Olson stumbled into Bluff, he was met by Gunnar Kaasen who headed out immediately, feeling that the weather would get worse before it got better. His lead dog, Balto, saved the team at one point when he hit open water – Balto wouldn't allow the rest of the team to proceed. At times when Kaasen couldn't see, Balto simply led the team in the right direction.

In the storm, Kaasen passed the next checkpoint and was two miles from it before familiar landmarks made him realize where he was. He kept going. He reached Point Safety at 2.00 A.M. The next driver, Ed Rhone, was sleeping soundly, thinking Kaasen was in Solomon waiting out the storm. Kaasen decided to keep going on to Nome.

That decision caused a controversy that raged for years. Was Kaasen worried about further delay? Or did he simply want the glory of being the man who brought the serum to Nome? At any rate, at 5.30 A.M., Monday morning, he and his exhausted team reached Nome. The trip of 674 miles was accomplished in 127½ hours, less than 5½ days.

The men of the relay had saved the town of Nome. For their efforts they each received $18.66 from a public subscription fund and $25.00 per day from the territory. They also received a citation from the governor and the H.K. Mumford Company sent medals to the drivers and $1,000 to Kaasen.

Many of those same teams hit the trail again when the second batch of serum arrived from Seattle. But the citations and the medals and certainly the $18.66 were not what drove those men to pit their courage against nature in the middle of winter. They knew that the lives of the citizens of Nome depended on them.

MIKE HENEY – THE IRISH PRINCE

»Give me enough snoose and dynamite and I'll build you a road to Hell.« Confident, boisterous words, yes. Unrealistic? Not when uttered by Mike Heney, the one man in Alaska's history who would build the »impossible« railroad. And he did it not once, but twice.

Michael J. Heney, the son of Irish immigrants, was born in Pembroke, Ontario, in 1864. From his early childhood, the sound of the railroad whistle and the fast moving engines puffing their way across the country meant adventure. While many boys only dreamed of »going railroading,« Mike did something about it. At age 16 he ran away from home to join the crews on the Canadian Pacific. Returning home to his worried parents, he waited until age 18 before setting off once again, this time with the Union Pacific. He worked his way to the west coast and when the Golden Spike completing the transcontinental railroad was driven, Mike found himself without a job. So he created one.

He went into the construction business for himself, starting with simple jobs and building his reputation. For the next 12 years, his life was one of construction. Finally, in 1887, he contracted and built the Seattle, Lake Shore and Eastern Railroad in western Washington – all 40 miles of it.

When word reached Seattle of the Klondike gold discoveries in Canada's Yukon Territory, Heney was drawn north; not to look for gold, but to build a railroad. He knew that there would be the need for a railroad to haul men and materials from the rugged Alaska coast to the mines.

After traveling north and exploring all the routes into the Klondike gold fields, Heney decided the White Pass out of Skagway would be the route for the railroad. Not that it would be an easy task to build. From sea level, the mountains rose to more than 10,000 feet. And there was a 3,000 foot rise in the first 20 miles. No, it was not an easy task at all.

A chance meeting in Skagway with the Close brothers, representatives of a London financial house, provided the necessary financing and the railroad work began.

It took 2,000 men working double shifts to complete the job in the 2 years Heney promised. Not only was the terrain difficult, supplies were 1,500 miles away and the winter snows so deep it often took days to clear the tracks to start construction again. And there was the ever-present danger from snowslides.

And there were other dangers. At Mile 15, the railroad had to pass directly across the face of a nearly perpendicular wall of granite about a half mile above the valley floor. The men had to be suspended by ropes from above in order to chisel the pathway and set dynamite charges. The men refused. Heney lowered himself down the wall with a rope around his waist and set the first charges himself. The work proceeded.

The good citizens of Skagway wanted the railroad, but they didn't want the tracks running through town where Heney wanted them. He solved the problem. A crew was organized and, in the dead of night the tracks were laid. The tracks stayed.

The completed railroad traversed more than 100 miles from Skagway to Whitehorse in the Yukon Territory. When it was completed, Heney's reputation as a railroad man was assured. He was also a fairly wealthy man. He could have enjoyed his reputation and the good life, but there was another road to build.

This time it was a road to copper instead of gold. Five railroads were actually started to the rich copper fields of the Copper River valley in Alaska's interior. The competition for the rights to the routes was worthy of a novel – and one was written by Rex Beach entitled »The Iron Trail.« The hero, Murray O'Neil, was in actuality Mike Heney, the Irish Prince. His nickname was the result of the fact that he was »a prince of a fellow.« Heney was always a soft touch, always willing to lend a helping hand. He was genuinely concerned about his men and their families.Thus the name and the resulting devotion of thousands of railroaders.

Heney looked over the situation from the coast of Alaska's Prince William Sound up the Copper valley and decided that the route to take was one branded »impossible« by others. This was the natural gateway formed by the Copper River. The problem was that at Mile 49 the Miles and Childs Glaciers faced each other, pouring hundreds of tons of ice into the river every year. Heney felt that »all« he had to do was blast through Abercrombie Canyon and conquer those glaciers. He filed for the route early with the General Land Office and set to work.

Heney may have had some money, but certainly not enough to finance a railroad of this magnitude. He knew that he would have to prove that his route was *the* route. His plan was simply to build far enough to convince the financiers to invest in his chosen route. It worked. In 1906, Heney sold out to the Guggenheim/Morgan Syndicate for the tidy sum of a quarter million dollars.

Heney's route did prove impossible to the syndicate's engineers, so Heney was called back and put in charge.

Nowhere along the route was the job an easy one. The line began at the new town of Cordova and extended across the flats, past Eyak Lake where two big cuts had to be made and on to Abercrombie Landing where three steel bridges had to be built across the flats and the mighty Copper River delta. More bridges followed. Land had to be filled. Blasting through Abercrombie Canyon required tons of dynamite. But the biggest challenge still lay at Mile 49. There they had to build what would become the »Million Dollar Bridge.« It had to be completed before spring when the glaciers began to move and the mighty icebergs came crashing down. And it had to be built strong enough to withstand the crush of tons of ice.

To make the project more difficult, the Copper River was full of rapids and shifting sandbars. And there was the Copper River wind – whistling down on the workers at velocities of 81 to 96 miles per hour.

Three support piers went in. Two 60 foot towers on each bank supported a 12 inch wide plank foot bridge. By May 11, 1910, the work was almost finished and then – the Miles Glacier began to move unexpectedly early. Ice four miles square and nine feet thick was being pushed against the bridge. Men with big chisels worked frantically to cut the ice from behind the pilings to relieve the pressure. They worked around the clock. The last bolt was driven at midnight on May 16, just hours ahead of an ice movement so thick it would have been impossible to fight. The bridge held.

On March 29, 1911, the final spike in the Copper River and Northwestern Railroad was driven, but Mike Heney wasn't there. His picture was, however, mounted on the front of his faithful Engine Number 50.

Heney had died six months before the road was finished. A shipwreck in 1909 in which he'd had to swim ashore in icy waters affected his health. He contracted pneumonia the next year and the pace he set and the elements in which he worked all took their toll. He died at age 45.

News of his death caused his men to mourn in the only way they knew. They plunged ahead with the road, determined to see that it was finished on time. At his funeral, General S.S. Burdett said it best: »He was truly one of the breed described by Kipling as ›Sons of Martha‹ who fill up the valleys, level the hills, bridge the torrents and tunnel the mountains that the sons of Mary may have a smooth road for their feet.«

There were many more, some just as well-known, many others who passed through without leaving their names, but all, as these few, left a mark on the land and a heritage that went on to add to the romance of the Great Land.

AVIATION AND THE STORY OF RAYMOND PETERSEN by Nan Elliot

The story of Alaska's settlement almost parallels the story of aviation. When the airplane was still a novelty in the rest of the world, it already was being put to work across the skies of Alaska. From Carl Ben Eielson's historic first mail flight in 1924 from Fairbanks to McGrath into the present, aviation has played an important part in the history of the state. And there have been many important aviators, pioneers whose stories and legends are as much a part of Alaska as the gold miners and dog mushers. One of these is Ray Petersen.

From his early days of barnstorming in an open cockpit plane »for a dollar a ride and the thrill of your life« to building one of Alaska's most prominent commercial airlines, Ray Petersen's life has been intimately interwoven with the history of aviation in this far northern frontier.

The airplane revolutionized the world. But its impact on Alaska has been, perhaps, one of the most dramatic. In the vastness of the 49th state where there are few roads, aerial highways provide the main transportation link between isolated villages and larger cities. Consequently, there are more planes per capita in this state than in any other.

Flying is not easy in this country; and flamboyancy is not the kind of characteristic that lasts too long. But in the 1930s when Ray Petersen steamed into Seward on the SS *Victoria,* the original »bush pilots,« those pioneer aviators, were literally, as they say, »flying by the seat of their pants.« Instrument flying was non-existent; charts and maps were useless; and a compass not always reliable. Pilots had their own special secrets for navigating. They learned to read the land, to sense the weather. In a country where ice and snow cover the earth more than half the year, they lived life on the edge, providing a service that soon became essential for survival. They cracked-up a lot of planes in those days, due to bad weather, lack of navigational equipment, primitive landing fields, or no landing fields at all. »The good pilots cracked-up planes, but never scratched a hair,« remembers Petersen. Until for a few of them, their luck ran out.

»Alaska aviation was performing a public service when they were still stunting and hauling movie stars around for publicity purposes in the rest of the United States, trying to get people to fly. People in the Lower 48s still rode trains. Flying did not come into its own until the jet age. From 1958 on, that's when mass transportation took to the air.

»But in Alaska, things were different,« recalls Petersen, once a cocky young kid from Chicago, who came to Alaska because he had heard that planes were *used* for something up there. In his 70's and

retired now, he is among the last of the old guard. But time has not diminished his brashness nor the confidence of those early days. Every once in a while as he re-lives the stories, the drama and characters become so alive he pauses to wipe a tear away. He allows the memories their due – a tribute to the people he knew along the way, and a way of life which never will be recaptured.

Ray Petersen was born in York, Nebraska, August 10, 1912. His folks homesteaded the Wyoming side of the Black Hills.

There are a lot of »firsts« in Petersen's life, but his earliest claim is having been the first passenger off at Chicago's O'Hare Airport. It was the summer of 1928. He was working on a farm on the outskirts of the city, the site of what is now one of the largest and busiest airports in the United States. A barnstormer asked for permission to practice in the farmer's hay field and took young Petersen up for a ride. It was not love at first sight, »but it sure seemed a lot easier work up there in the air, than down in the fields cutting hay.«

Whether or not that was the initial inspiration, young Ray dropped out of school after the tenth grade and took up flying. He soloed his first plane at the age of 17 and got his commercial pilot's license one year later. License in hand, he leased an airport in Wisconsin and with one plane, an OX-5 powered Command-Aire, he went into business, giving rides and teaching a few dedicated students to fly. »After Lindbergh flew the Atlantic in 1927, there was a big boom in aviation across the country. My predecessors had gone broke. Later I understood why. Mostly people came out, not to ride, but to rubberneck – to watch a few spins and loops and barrel rolls and, maybe, if they were lucky, a crash. That would have been the icing on the cake. Those people were just out there to see you get killed.

»One of my students told me he had been to Alaska and up there they used airplanes to do all kinds of work. It was the best way to get around. Well, that sounded like a good idea to me.« By working in a slot machine factory in Chicago, Petersen earned his passage north and arrived in the port of Seward on April 1, 1934.

Aviation had taken hold of the frontier in the late 1920s. Even though it wasn't cheap – a one-way ticket between Anchorage and Bethel was $750 then – by 1934, except for a few isolated mail routes, it had virtually put the dog teams out of business. The airplane took three hours to cover distances it took three weeks to travel by dog team. When Petersen arrived, there were 58 planes in the whole Territory, primarily servicing gold miners and the fishing industry.

The discovery of gold in the Canadian Klondike in 1896 had brought tens of thousands north following the lure of glittering fortune. That stampede opened the door into Alaska's gold fields. It was not long after, that gold was discovered on the Seward Peninsula and the Territory became peopled with prospectors. By 1900 Nome was a tent city with more than 20,000 prospectors working the shores. As men struck gold, towns sprang up almost overnight all over Alaska: Iditarod, Hope, Fortuna Ledge, Ruby, Wiseman, Pedro Creek.

»Aviation completely changed the complexion and economics of Alaska,« explains the pioneer flyer. »In the 1930s, the airplane caused another gold rush which kept up until the beginning of World War II when all gold mining had to stop as not important to the war effort.

»You see, until the plane came, mining was done by large dredges or by pick and shovel. The season lasted until the rivers froze up. So miners spent the winter months indoors due to the expense and hardship of long dog team travel.

»The airplane changed all that. It could fly crews in and out in a matter of hours. They could go to Seattle for the winter. They did not have to be boarded or bored. And, believe me, out at those mines the long winter months were boring. Furthermore, planes could transport equipment such as bulldozers, pumps, and elevated tressels, making it possible to mine otherwise uneconomical ground. If they broke down, the airplane could bring in spare parts fast.«

In the 1930s, Fairbanks was the popular center of aviation. It was easier to operate airplanes out of that city – prior to instrument flying – since it was not ringed by mountain ranges like Anchorage. But Petersen ended up in Anchorage and spent the first six months as a »flying trapper and prospector.« His next job was with Star Air Service, the predecessor to Alaska Airlines, which many years later would become his prime competitor.

»We were servicing the Lucky Shot Mine on Willow Creek, about a halfhour flight in a Curtiss Robin from Merrill Field in Anchorage. We also had three Belancas. And there were four pilots. We never hurt anybody, but we sure wrecked a lot of planes from September to February that year. Each of the Belancas cracked-up twice, mainly due to poor landing conditions. Consequently, we had the best planes because they were always being rebuilt to new standards.«

When he hired on, he had told the boss »I won't kill myself, but I won't promise not to damage a plane.« His employer told him »Sonny, there's no guarantees in this business.« One week later to the hour he cracked-up his second plane in a heavy fog on the Merrill Field beacon.

With that, he was grounded. In those days, a pilot worked on commission. If he cracked up a plane, he simply had to wait until it was fixed. Not inclined to wait, Petersen headed west for Bethel, the transportation and supply center of southwest Alaska. At the mouth of the Kuskokwim River, the town was in a strategic location. It could be reached by ocean-going ships and barges. From there river boats could take men and equipment into interior Alaska.

In 1935 on borrowed money, Petersen and a partner started Bethel Airways Corporation. At that time there was only one other flying service in town. »Bethel had about 500 people. Of the white population – about one-fifth of the town – the main forces were traders, Moravian missionaries, and government school teachers and nurses. So things were lively. There was plenty of conflict and a lot of bickering going on which was good entertainment.« Petersen chuckled at the memory.

To get his new business off the ground, he returned to Chicago to buy a plane and ferry it back to Bethel. In Seattle, he met up with Noel Wien from Fairbanks who had just flown down the photographs of the Wiley Post/Will Rogers crash. (While vacationing in Alaska in 1935, the celebrated pilot and the American humorist crashed near Barrow and were killed). »Noel always claimed he flew the first passengers from Seattle to Fairbanks. And he was half right. He took the Lomens of Nome in his newly purchased Ford Tri-Motor. But I was flying right alongside him in a seven-passenger, single-engine Travel Aire with two passengers – a young Eskimo fellow whose father was a trapper on the Lower Kuskokwim and Johnny ›Muskrat‹ Schwegler, a well known fur trader who used to trade up and down the Siberian coast during the early 1920s.«

The flying service went belly up when both Petersen and his partner cracked-up their planes two years later; one at a gold miner's landing field and the other in a collision with a fishing boat on Bristol Bay. His partner tossed-in the towel and left the country. But Petersen stayed in Bethel. He thought he would try his hand in gold. »In 1936, everyone wanted to be a gold miner. But I discovered it didn't pay the bills.« So he borrowed more money, thumbed a ride on a trader's ship, came into Anchorage, bought another plane – a Ryan B-1, a derivative of the *Spirit of St. Louis* – and returned to Bethel to make good on his debts.

With the purchase of that plane was born Ray Petersen's Flying Service, the original company which eventually led, through several mergers, to the airline known today as Wien Air Alaska.

When the Japanese bombed Pearl Harbor and the United States entered the war, gold mining in Alaska came to a near standstill. Flying in the Territory changed considerably for the war effort.

»Pilots in Alaska had ›Double A-1 Priority‹ which

47

meant we could commandeer almost anything except a new plane or engine, and we had complete draft deferments as did our mechanics. Originally, I think they were planning on making Alaska a bombing base for the Pacific. But the weather was so terrible here, it never worked out. In the Aleutian Islands, nine out of ten of the pilots killed in the war died as a result of weather accidents not combat.«

Petersen flew military charters, mapping and weather missions for government agencies; and medical equipment, as well as patients to hospitals, in addition to ferrying supplies to civilian Alaskans scattered throughout the Territory as he had done in the past. Although gold wasn't being mined, platinum was considered a strategic mineral for the war, and he continued to take care of the platinum mines 120 miles south of Bethel at Goodnews Bay. The miners there had initially bankrolled Ray Petersen's Flying Service and the aviator had done so well he could service them now with five planes.

Although he kept a base in Bethel, during the war Petersen moved into Anchorage and pulled together four other air companies under the same roof, maintaining ticketing and ground service for their joint operations.

»At the end of the war it was obvious that we were going to have to get instrument equipment. The army had in surplus literally hundreds of C-47s. The C-47 was the military version of the DC-3. With its cargo door it was a good airplane for our use, and you could buy it for about $20,000, at $3,000 down, and a dollar a week. So we were able to get into an instrument operation and stop this business of sometimes waiting a week or two to get through the passes. This was a great step forward.« (Anchorage at the head of Cook Inlet is ringed by mountain ranges – the Chugach to the east, the Alaska Range to the west and north. In order to fly west, through the mountains toward Bethel, one has to navigate through one of three passes, and these can be wicked if the weather closes in.)

But there was another problem, Petersen explained. »The airplanes were too big for our services. Here I was operating a schedule of three flights a week into Bethel carrying passengers and cargo in a Stinson eight-passenger Tri-Motor. That airplane carried about 2,000 pounds. Then along comes this DC-3 that carried three times as much, and cost that much more to run. This, along with increased federal regulations, created a real problem. I had to get operating on instruments.

»We had never received any federal help on the airlines up here. Down in the states, why good night, they were shoving millions of dollars into the airlines to get them started and here we were providing an essential service for years and never got any government help. And really, we never asked for it. We didn't want too much interference.

»To start with, we *had* to fill the airplanes. For example, we reduced the freight rates from about 40 cents a pound to 13 cents a pound between Anchorage and Bethel to at least fill the space with freight. Well, this suddenly made it possible for people to get fresh eggs and fresh fruit into all those points. But economically it would not support us. So we applied for federal subsidy to cover these lower rates and to stimulate traffic.«

In the years that followed, Petersen brought several air services together along with their mail contracts, which in turn provided the federal subsidy.

The new, combined air service was called Northern Consolidated and it also took passengers and cargo to Seattle. The trip was long, with at least one refueling stop, and meant bucking notoriously gray Southeastern weather and darting through the clouds into Yakutat, Juneau or Ketchikan. »Legally we could not run a regular schedule to Seattle. We had to run on what they called a casual, occasional and infrequent basis. So, we would run a schedule to Seattle to beat heck for a couple of months, and then we would have to break it. We could not legally lead the public to believe that they could depend on a reasonable and regular service. So it became unreasonable, irregular, casual, occasional and infrequent.«

Later, larger Outside airlines were granted the routes by the federal government.

By 1958, Northern Consolidated had expanded into prop jets and in 1968 the company brought in jets. »After years of negotiating with Douglas and Boeing, Boeing finally came up with the best plane for our needs, the 737 with the gravel kits so you could operate it off landing fields in Alaska and not kick gravel up into the engines, large cargo doors, and that could go nonstop to Seattle or round trip between Prudhoe Bay or Barrow and Anchorage. We finally got the airplane we needed.

»But once again I was confronted with the problem of strong enough routes to support the bigger airplane. That's when we merged Wien into Northern Consolidated in 1968. At that time, Wien served the north: Fairbanks, Nome, Kotzebue, Barrow, and Whitehorse in the Yukon. We bought it from Sig (Wien) who had taken over the business in 1940 from Noel (his brother). We called it Wien Consolidated because we wanted to keep that Wien name going. Noel Wien had come up here in 1924, and we wanted to keep that good name alive.

»And I don't know where we had a lapse of intelligence – my wife never forgave me for this ... a lot of people actually didn't – when we called it Wien Air Alaska.

»But Alaska has changed a great deal in the last

decade. When we merged with Wien the combined business grossed $10 million a year. At the time I retired in 1978, the airline was making $70 million a year. Today, it's a $150 million a year business. Of course, there's a lot more people traveling now, too.«

When Raymond Petersen retired from the company, he looked back over a career in aviation which had seen dramatic changes: from open cockpit stunt flying to mass transportation in the jet age; from a single aviator's flying service to the development of major airlines; from the tent city of Anchorage to the high rises of present-day downtown. In Alaska he is the founding father of an aviation empire.

A leather-helmeted and be-goggled goose is the symbol of the airline familiar throughout the state as »The Wien Bird.« This is an achievement he reflects on with pride. But asked what his most powerful memories are from his years in the flying business, he does not hesitate. »Those first six years in Bethel, that was really the beginning.« What was it like to fly in those days? »If the weather was flyable, you flew. The weather was very changeable, just like it is today. You would have a forty-mile-an-hour wind from the south and thawing, and tomorrow you would have a wind from the north and it would be −10°F. Tough weather country. Nothing has improved. But we didn't have any instruments. You had to know your country. It was easy to get lost.

»You didn't go out with maps and charts and lay out a dead reckoning course. Some of the early Pan-Am pilots did that and got themselves beautifully lost. This is what I did, and I suppose all the rest of them did too. We were reluctant to give away all our secrets. You see, no one trained us. Here's the airplane. Go! No one took me through these passes, I had to find them myself. For years the old Iditarod Trail was an absolute must. You couldn't find Rainy Pass without it. When that trail began to get obliterated, that's when we needed instruments. You couldn't get through that pass in marginal weather. You didn't have anything to go by. You could fly up the wrong valley awful easy.

»The Iditarod Trail was absolutely vital. The old dog trails were the best navigational instruments we had, like railroads were for pilots down in the Lower states.«

As an example, Petersen describes one trip from Flat to Crooked Creek as a young, inexperienced pilot. »I had one passenger with me I'd brought from Anchorage. He lived over at Akiak and he was a pipesmoker. We took off and it was snowing and you couldn't see very well. But I had a dog trail to follow between Flat and Crooked Creek. When I got on the Kuskokwim River it was easy to follow the river in bad weather, so I didn't think anything of it. I couldn't

see very far, but I could see that dog trail. Pretty soon I smelled smoke. Old Joe was smoking his pipe and had knocked a spark loose. It had got caught in the old wicker seat cushion.

»Well, you could throw a cat through the airplane in those days. There was no insulation. You just dressed warm when you flew. You didn't have to worry about carbon monoxide poisoning then 'cause there was lots of ventilation. But that breeze also fanned the flames. I'm trying to follow the dog trail with rolling white hills and snow everywhere, and I handed back the fire extinguisher and yelled, »Joe, put that fire out and be sure it is out.« He squirted at it and I thought we were finished with that when pretty soon I smelled smoke again. This was getting serious. There was no place to land.

»I grabbed the fire extinguisher, wheeled around to douse the smoke and flames, turning back only to steady the plane. But during that time the plane veered off course and I lost the dog trail.

»Now things were really serious. Which way was which? It's all white out there and your compass is not very reliable anyway. So I had to learn real fast – fly your watersheds. And you don't go upstream 'cause you're going in the mountains. But with the snow and ice, how do you know which is downstream?

»I got real observant. I noticed the way the trees had fallen in the crick. When they fell, the current pulled them downstream. I had to make a quick decision, and I had never observed that before. So I headed down the crick into the George River and I knew I was okay because that flows into the Kuskokwim. We got into Crooked Creek and I breathed a sigh of relief.

»You see, I had always followed the dog trails. The dog trail was staked and you followed the stakes. But it got complicated, because there were those big lakes. Flying in bad weather you would go from stake to stake, set about 500 feet apart, and pretty soon you run out of stakes, because you were crossing a big lake. Well, what they did with the dog teams was that they would build tripods on the lakes. But the dog teams had stopped running when the airplane really took hold in the Territory. The stakes were still there, but the tripods had long since fallen into the lakes during spring thaw.

»Suddenly you were over this big expanse and nothing to navigate by. So you would take a dead reckoning across the lake, and when you were on the other side you began bracketing (flying from side to side) until you picked up the stakes again.

»And that's the way you flew this country.«

Winter temperatures fall as low as −51°F and beyond in the interior; often thick layers of icefog blanket the plains and river valleys.

Aurora Borealis in a curtain form; northern lights in all shapes and in many colors can be frequently seen – and heard – in spring and fall in the interior and far north of Alaska, sometimes even further south. The University of Alaska in Fairbanks is one of the world's best equipped research centers for this phenomenon.

Noon dusk at Christmas time in downtown Fairbanks. This lively city, ranking second in population, is the center of Alaska's heartland. Unlike many other flourishing gold rush settlements, Fairbanks continues to prosper as a trade and transportation center for the entire northern region.

In the frontier city of Nome one can recapture the spirit of Alaska's gold rush era at the turn of the century, when some 20,000 people from all over the world followed the call of gold, first discovered in Anvil Creek and on the beaches of the Bering Sea; old gold dredges are evidence of those times, but today gold mining is again becoming a lucrative operation. Like many other towns and villages at the Bering Sea, Nome is often plagued by vicious storms.

From the Prudhoe Bay oil fields, largest in North America, more than 1.5 million barrels per day are transported via the Trans-Alaska pipeline to the Gulf port of Valdez. With a diameter of 48 inches, this once-in-a-century 800 mile-long construction was built under the harshest of climatic conditions within a 3-year period and put into service in June of 1977.

▷

Spruce trees and taiga in the colors of autumn.

Rock ptarmigan, mother and her chicks; the willow ptarmigan is Alaska's »state bird.«

Arctic cotton, near Saint Marys.

Icebergs, calved off the Columbia Glacier, one of southcentral Alaska's many natural attractions, and kayaker in Valdez Arm of Prince William Sound.

Two anglers amidst glacial icebergs, waiting for the next big catch.

John Hopkins Glacier, one of the several tidewater glaciers in Glacier Bay that have, in modern times, receded at a pace never before recorded.

Ruggedly coastlined Kodiak Island, a giant rock of 3,588 sq. miles and site of the first Russian fur trade settlement in the 18th century. Its only larger city is Kodiak, center of the commercial fishing and fish processing industry. Famous for its Kodiak bears, its huge runs of king and red salmon and its king crabs. One of the many wild streams is Karluk River, up which each year the salmon struggle overcoming numerous falls on the way to their spawning grounds.

The blanket toss, a game still popular today, was originated by Eskimo hunters who used this means to spot distant prey across the ridges of arctic sea ice. It is also performed for visitors in Barrow and Kotzebue in the summertime.

When the Eskimo whalers return to Point Hope after a successful hunt, the whale meat is cut up with the *ulu*, the Eskimo woman's knife; pieces of the outer skin layers are called *muktuk* and are considered a delicacy.

Meeting the mail plane on the frozen Kashunuk River at Chevak, a small Yup'ik(-Eskimo) village; snowmobiles are today's winter transportation vehicles for the young and old.

NATIVES OF ALASKA by Lael Morgan

Today Alaska's aboriginal people are referred to broadly as Natives, distinguished from Caucasians who were born in the state by a capital »n«, but the all-inclusive term is misleading in that it covers people of many different races, geographies and philosophies.

Early explorers discovered Alaska to be inhabited by five separate tribes or nations with no common language, and lifestyles and traditions that varied with the vast terrain they occupied.

The barren arctic tundra in the extreme north was (and is) the domain of the Inupiat Eskimo whose remarkable adaptation to the world's toughest environment has wrongly become the stereotype for all Alaskans.

The Inupiat developed ingenious fur clothing so impervious to cold that modern science has yet to better it. They invented sunglasses to protect themselves from the blinding glare of snow in the bright spring sunlight and learned to kindle fire by sparking iron pyrites with quartz to burn seal oil for light and heat during the dark winter days. On the coast they devised methods of hunting from treacherous moving ice floes which enabled them to take bowhead whales of 50 or 60 tons. They discovered how to kill polar bears by feeding them lethally bent pieces of whalebone encased in blubber and, inland, they learned to corral wild caribou and hunted them also with snares and bows and arrows.

Unlike Eskimos of the eastern arctic, Alaska Inupiat did not use snow houses except as emergency shelters from storms. Instead they built sod dwellings so snug they could be heated by simple stone oil lamps in the dead of winter. They believed in good and evil spirits and ceremoniously laid their dead to rest on platforms above the ground. They also learned to mark the passing of time by the sun and stars, established 12 months to the year and could count into the hundreds.

Although generally nomadic, the wealth of the sea sometimes afforded them the luxury of permanent settlement and one of their sites on a game-rich spit in the Chukchi Sea is the oldest continuously inhabited site known in North America.

The Yup'ik people, Eskimo cousins of the Inupiat to the southwest, shared much in common with the northerners but could not understand their language. Their barren tundra could not support as much wildlife as that of the Inupiat and no giant whales swam in the shallow seas off their coasts, but the Kuskokwim and Yukon river systems afforded them a fine transportation network for their fleet – sealskin covered kayaks – and their waters abounded with fish. Because of their usually dependable food source, Yup'ik people tended to be less nomadic than their northern neighbors and developed a more sophisticated sociocultural system evolving around a central kashgee – men's living quarters and ceremonial house – in every village. Since fur was less readily available in southwestern Alaska, the Yup'ik utilized colorful bird skins for clothing and fish skins for boots. The designs of their seamstresses were often intricate and they used carved ivory, bone or animal teeth as well as feathers for decoration.

The Yup'ik world was created by the raven, according to their thinking, and their religion was strong under the leadership of powerful shamans. Their numerical system went only to ten and some regarded them as backward in comparison to other Native groups for they clung stubbornly to their traditions, yet Yup'ik Eskimos were the only Natives to devise their own written language after the coming of outsiders.

Farther southwest, the Aleuts claimed the longest archipelago of small islands in the world and much of the neighboring Alaska Peninsula. Although thought to be of Eskimo stock, they did not speak the same language as the Yup'iks or Inupiat and their lifestyle was vastly different, for the Aleuts were a maritime people of unmatched skill. Their living came from storm-prone seas which they plied with marvelously crafted kayaks and skin boats. Hunting with cleverly designed throwing boards, spears and sometimes poisoned darts, they subsisted on an unusually wide variety of sea mammals including large whales. They sewed warm, waterproof garments from the intestines of seals and walrus, could navigate by the stars and often covered hundreds of miles of open sea.

Because they had access to few fur bearing animals, they often fashioned clothing out of bird skins and sometimes of woven grasses which they also used for making mats and baskets. They developed an intricate knowledge of anatomy and medicine, performed surgery, used suturing and mummified their dead.

Aleuts learned to make fire with sulfur and quartz but driftwood was highly valued on their treeless islands and they seldom wasted fire for cooking or to heat their sod houses and their existence was spartan. Newborn babies were baptised in the sea, regardless of season, and early explorers were astonished to note these people walking shoeless in winter snows.

The Aleuts believed in many spirits and had a special cult for whale hunters who were of high status but mysteriously died young. They organized loosely structured governments headed by a toyon or chief on each island and warred constantly among themselves and with other tribes.

In strong contrast were the Athabascan Indians who dwelled in interior forests, occupying only a small stretch of coast in the area of Cook Inlet. These were restless hunters who traveled in small bands and family groups, constantly following the game, with only a minimum of tribal organization. In summer they paddled birchbark canoes and sometimes employed dog teams along the river banks to pull their boats; in winter they snowshoed or hitched dogs to pull birchwood sleds.

They hunted with bows, arrows and snares and lived occasionally in underground houses, but more often in skin tents. They wore clothing of caribou and moose skins and parkas of marten, beaver and wolf. They had an eye for design, used fringes for decoration and also porcupine quills and when trade goods became available the women became famous for their beautiful beadwork.

Their religion is little understood but seems to have involved songs and speeches addressed to spirits of nature. Their taboos were many and they observed puberty and death with elaborate celebration. Occasionally they left their dead where they fell but in some areas cremation was a custom and a system of burial with prized possessions became popular in later years.

The Athabascan language was difficult with many dialects and, strangely, of the same stock and still intelligible to the Navajos who lived much farther south. The Athabascans were a minority people in Alaska but fierce fighters and they were successfully expanding their territory to accommodate their growing numbers at the time of discovery.

Most sophisticated of Alaskans were the Tlingit Indians and their Haida cousins of Southeastern who, because of bountiful fish and game, lush forests and a relatively mild climate, had considerably more time than others to develop a strong tribal system and some highly artistic skills.

Their population was divided into two main clans and numerous smaller ones, ruled by strong chiefs and shamans. Unlike most other Alaska Natives who were socialistic, Southeastern Indians judged a man's worth by accumulated wealth and their chiefs and first families were forever trying to outdo one another in staging eleborate give-away parties called potlatches.

About one third of the Tlingit and Haida population was made up of slaves taken through war or trade. Copper, worked in large plates, and a rare shell called dentalium also served as a medium of exchange and an indicator of wealth.

Their weapons, which included copper knives, were superior to those of other Alaskans and they were merciless warriors of considerable skill.

The Southeastern Indians lived in ornamented wooden tribal houses in well-ordered villages and traveled in fast-moving wooden canoes which could accommodate up to 50 warriors. They learned to spin and weave the wool of mountain goats, to work copper, wood and stone; and with the introduction of steel tools their artisans began to carve huge heraldry totems for which their tribes soon became famous. Their music and dance were remarkably inventive and their ceremonial clothing, which included woven blankets and finely carved headresses, was spectacular.

Although long debated, it is generally thought the forebears of all Alaskans were migrants who came from Asia over a land bridge which spanned the Bering Sea some 65,000 to 35,000 years ago and also existed during the later Wisconsin ice age (from 28,000 to 10,000 years ago) until submerged by seas advancing from glacial melt.

Anthropologists have discovered many elements linking the oldest cultures to those of northern and central Asia but recent digs along the route of the Trans-Alaska pipeline and elsewhere in the interior may establish immigration from the east as well.

Whatever their origins, Alaska's first people thrived in the resource rich territory and numbered about 70,000 at the time of their discovery by the civilized world. Despite the vast distances that separated them, there was growing commerce among Alaskan groups as well as trade with Siberia. Iron was becoming known to them through Siberian Eskimos who traded with Russian neighbors and their cultures were advancing.

»Left alone, the Natives of Alaska might have unfolded into as bright a civilization as that of Europe,« speculated 19th century historian Hubert Howe Bancroft who studied the remnants of their culture. »They were already well advanced and still rapidly advancing towards it when they were so unmercifully stricken down.«

In 1742 Russian Tsar Peter the Great dispatched Vitus Bering to lead an expedition east on what is now known as the »last great voyage of discovery« and despite misfortune which caused the loss of one ship and cost the life of Bering himself, the crew returned to confirm existence of the Aleutian Chain and the Alaska mainland, bringing with them a rich bounty of furs as tangible evidence of the wealth and potential of the new land.

There followed hords of ruthless Russian traders who plundered Aleut territory, enslaving the Natives and forcing them to pay taxes in fur.

»Fortunately for the Indians of the North, it was contrary to the interests of white people to kill them in order to obtain the skins of their animals for, with a few trinkets, (the white man) could procure what otherwise would require long and severe labor to obtain,« historian Bancroft noted. »The policy, therefore, of the great fur trading companies has been to cherish the Indians as their best hunters, to live in peace with them, to heal their ancient feuds and to withhold from them intoxicating liquors.«

But history also recorded that the population of the Aleutian Islands dwindled from 10,000 or 20,000 to 2,000 in the first 50 years of Russian stewardship and other areas were hard hit. Using the Aleutians as way stations, the outsiders moved steadily toward the Alaska mainland and despite fierce resistance, established bases in the territory of the Tlingit of Southeastern, among the southwestern Eskimos and the Athabascans of Cook Inlet and the Yukon.

The Alaskans fought back but, although no treaties were ever signed and the Natives never officially surrendered, they eventually settled into coexistence with the Russians and grew increasingly dependent on them for trading goods.

Plagued by wars with other world powers and dwindling returns on their Alaska colony, Russia sold it to the United States in 1867 without consent or even the knowledge of the Native people, but a memorandum dispatched by the Russians shortly after the signing of their treaty of cession made it clear the transaction did not involve land title but rather Russian improvements and the right to trade and govern.

Major John Tidball, one of the first U.S. military commanders in the newly acquired territory, reported that the Indians expressed the »same villainous traits of character« found among the warring Indians of the United States. In light of the fact there were no more than 2,000 whites to an estimated 25,000 aborigines, it was felt that a display of military force was needed, but even after most of the U.S. Army troops were withdrawn from Alaska to quell Indian uprisings elsewhere, white fears proved groundless. The Natives were too busy fighting for their own survival to bother newcomers.

Beyond considerations for defense, America's early Alaska Indian policy was one of neglect and in 1889 the commander of a government revenue cutter reported the coastal Eskimos to be »in a most degraded state, physically, mentally and spiritually« as the result of contact with outsiders.

»Each visit of a whaling ship was followed by riot and drunkenness; the women were carried off to serve the lusts of the sailors and officers. Although under the flag of the United States, there was nothing but chaos and paganism.«

Nor was this an isolated case. Dispirited by large numbers of whalers and traders, weakened by newly introduced diseases, increasing numbers of Alaskans sought comfort in alcohol (then a novelty) and village life was disrupted.

Since the government showed no interest in helping, salvation was left to missionaries. Strongest among them was Sheldon Jackson, a Presbyterian who valued education as being second only to God and vigorously sought schooling for Native children so they might be assimilated into the American mainstream.

When the government refused to fund schools, Jackson divided the territory among interested church groups; the Baptists getting Kodiak and Cook Inlet; the Episcopalians working the Yukon and lower Arctic; the Methodists moving into the Aleutian Chain; the Moravians going to the Kuskokwim; the Quakers getting the Kotzebue area; the Congrationalists settling at Cape Prince of Wales; and the Presbyterians taking Southeastern and the north Arctic Coast.

Jackson also introduced reindeer herding in many areas with the hopes of giving the Natives some economic base and eventually succeeded in getting government appropriations for both animal husbandry and education. His efforts proved beneficial in many areas where missionaries and teachers were humanitarians or at least good at the practice of medicine, but acculturation was their watchword and their proselytizing made considerable inroads on valued traditions.

The decimation was by no means as complete, however, as in other areas such as the western states or south seas where »civilizing« efforts were directed, for Alaskans were protected by the very element that had long been their enemy – the harshness of the country. No matter how much outsiders put down Native cultures, Alaskans saw that by maintaining them they could survive well beyond the endurance of the average newcomer. And because of this knowledge, most developed cagey distrust for the reservation system in which the government from time to time attempted to corral them.

An Athabascan chief who attended a hearing on reservations held by the federal government in 1915 articulated the Native viewpoint:

»You told me that you were our people's friend, and you did not like to see us get into any kind of mischief. You stated to me that anything we want we should talk to you about now. Therefore, I tell you that we are people that are always on the go, and I believe if we are put in one place we shall die-off like rabbits. I tell you also that if you wanted to do anything good for us, you must select somebody for us who was truthful and not untruthful.

»I ask you not to let the white people come near us. Let us live our own lives in the customs we know. If we were on government ground we could not keep the white people away.«

About 1929 some of the more sophisticated villages began to incorporate as cities and in 1934 Congress passed the Indian Reorganization Act providing eco-

66

nomic assistance to tribes so they could charter corporations.

In 1935 the Tlingit-Haida Jurisdictional Act gave Indians the right to sue. A year later these people, led by a Tlingit lawyer, filed suit against the U.S. government for $80 million in lost timberland but the case was shuttled about the courts for three decades before settlement and for the most part the Native population was ignored.

During World War II, however, the federal government was forced by lack of troops, to leave Alaska's northern coasts undefended and Natives from remote areas organized and served as a protective military unit without pay, proving to be exemplary soldiers. Others joined regular military branches and returned from combat with records of distinction which earned the respect of white neighbors.

Shortly thereafter, the Alaska Territorial Legislature passed an anti-discrimination law (the first in the nation), which called for equal treatment of Natives and whites in business establishments and public places.

Yet Alaska Natives remained among the world's poorest people with minimum or no government services. Their infant mortality rate was higher than that of Indians. Life expectancy in the arctic seldom exceeded 27 years. And they had no legal title to land on which they had lived for centuries.

The turning point came in 1958 when the Atomic Energy Commission developed a plan to blast a harbor off Alaska's northwest coast to demonstrate peaceful uses of the atom. It failed to take into account some 800 Eskimos who lived in the area, however, and only belatedly offered to move them to a city housing project.

In protest, Eskimo leaders backed by the Association of American Indian Affairs, held an unprecedented meeting which they called »Inupiat Paitot« – the people's heritage.

Until this time there had been little communication among Native communities and even less between Natives and whites. To counter, Inupiat Paitot members founded a crusading, statewide newspaper, »Tundra Times.« It was published by Howard Rock, a well-known artist and one of the few Eskimos who had managed to obtain a college education, and through his efforts the fledgling statewide Native movement gained a powerful voice. The atomic testing project was quickly scrapped and »Tundra Times« concentrated its efforts on bringing to light discrimination problems which were widespread despite legislation for equal rights.

Then, in 1962, there began a push for settlement of Native land claims. During this period oil companies filed leases covering the Athabascan settlements of Minto and Nenana and the state government started making tentative land selections in the area under a provision of the Alaska Statehood Act which allowed Alaska to acquire a »dowry« of land from the federal government. Neither state nor federal officials paid any attention to Native claims, but the »Tundra Times« helped its people file suit, raising question of ownership.

Soon the state was blanketed by Native land claims and in 1966 the Secretary of Interior invoked a land freeze, stopping all development until the question of ownership could be resolved.

Also in 1966 a group of young, alert Alaskan Natives entered politics and even remote villages became politically aware. Natives then numbered about 50,000, making up one-fifth of the state's electorate, and they began to exercise their vote, swinging statewide elections to candidates who favored their causes. Native leaders organized a strong legislative voting block and in 1967 pushed through a bill promising a state royalty to Indians, Eskimos and Aleuts if the federal government would settle their land claims.

Shortly thereafter a statewide coalition of Natives organized to push for Congressional settlement. Outsiders predicted the Alaska Federation of Natives would not survive because it required close cooperation among aborigines who had warred for centuries. However, the Natives managed to overcome barriers of diversified language and philosophy and in 1971 gained the largest federal settlement on record; one billion dollars and 44 million acres of land.

The settlement was different from others made on aboriginal people in that the administration was left to the Natives themselves, who were to organize 13 regional corporations to manage and increase their wealth. Village corporations also were formed with Native residents as voting stockholders.

At the time of the settlement, more than 70 percent of Alaska Natives were dependent on hunting and fishing and the transition to a money-based economy was by no means immediate. Many still depend on old ways. In some areas regional corporations have not been successful, but others have prospered paying dividends to their stockholders and investing carefully in what appears to be a secure future while working to preserve their culture. Independent of the claims settlement, Native people have progressed rapidly through broadened educational and employment opportunities. Housing, transportation and communications in their remote areas are improving rapidly. With better care, Native health statistics are now almost on par with those of the rest of the nation and Native populations are expanding to the point they will soon equal or better census figures at the time of discovery.

Native voting blocks are still strong and since

Natives constitute the largest group of private land owners in Alaska, they are in a prime position to influence future development. Yet, surprisingly, despite rapid moves into the 20th century, the watchword is no longer assimilation.

From the heart of the Native movement there emerged a new pride in traditional cultures and a desire to preserve them. While taking a major place in the nation's capitalistic society, Alaska Natives are also very aware of their own unique heritage and with luck and patience they may yet have the best of both worlds.

NATIVE VERSES FROM ALASKA
Inupiat Eskimo

According to the ancient whalers of Tikiqaq which is now the village of Point Hope, Allingnuk is the Dweller of the Moon who has the power to allot talismen to whalers for good luck in their hunt. Thus as spring approaches the wives of village whaling captains chant to the »man in the moon« pleading for a successful hunt for their husbands.

Oh Allingnuk, Dweller of the Moon,
Allingnuk, great and generous giver of whales –
I, Nikuwanna, whose wife I am of Killikvuk,
A young and hopeful new whaler of Tikiqaq,
Implore thee for thy life-giving gift.
With the aid and lightness of these, the feathers,
May the spirit of my being rise and
Take upon a flight
This vessel I hold aloft and come nigh thee
So thou mayest drop a talisman or two of whales
Into this, the clear water of the pond.
Do this, O great Allingnuk,
So every being of Tikiqaq may dance and feast
For thee
At the close of the great season of whaling –
Oh Allingnuk, Dweller of the Moon,
Allingnuk, great and generous giver of whales –
I, Nikuwanna, whose wife I am of Killikvuk,
A young and hopeful new whaler of Tikiqaq
Implore thee for thy life-giving gift.

Modern Inupiat

Willie Hensley, raised by nomadic Eskimos, came to the fore early in the ranks of Native leaders and is today chairman of Alaska's only Native owned bank and a respected businessman. He has never forgotten his roots, however, and offers this explanation of modern Eskimo thinking.

In days of sod and snow
No armor stood before
The naked Eskimo as
Cannon boomed and prayers
Combined to mold
A cold philosophy.

Contemporary Inupiat

In Kiana, Willie Hensley wrote down the following verses.

WILL THE WARMTH OF APRIL EVER COME AGAIN?

The howling winds beat about
My fur-clad limbs
As stinging sands of snow
Whip about the milky universe.

Great gusts of might attempt to
Bring me to the ground;
Around the snowbanks huskies
Huddle chained together.

Cold darkness night and day enshrouds
My mind and will,
As dreams of April warmth,
Return to ease the loss of spring.

In April the golden sun appears
And cracks the winter grip:
Will the warmth of April ever come
Again to me?

Traveling Yup'iks

Edward W. Nelson was one of the few outsiders to see the Yup'ik culture at its height. In the late 1890s he traveled the lower Yukon River and had luck enough to be invited to an elaborate »Feast for the Dead« which drew Eskimos from a wide area and lasted almost two weeks. This was an occasion for much song and dance and Nelson wrote down and translated several of the Yup'ik songs. The first tells of the boat trip made by a group of guests with their sled dogs. The second is a song of mourning to mark the occasion.

We will sing a song
We will go down the current
The waves will rise
The waves will fall
The dogs will growl at us

Come, my brother
Return to us again.
We wait for you;
Come, brother come,
Our mother, come back to us
Return once more
Return our father;
We wait for you
Come back to us,
And we, who are lonely,
Will give you food.

Modern Yup'ik Verse

St. Mary's Catholic High School, a boarding school on the Yukon River, was long the only choice for Yup'ik youngsters who wished to continue their education and is still a favored choice for many because of its fine reputation. In 1976 students of this institution published »Through Yup'ik Eyes/Yupiit Lingitgun,« a marvelous book of poetry and photographs by students. The following verses come from this collection and are by Mary Lou Tony.

I LONG TO FOLLOW

The sun is rising,
The river, yet in dark
Is the cold blue-silver of steel –
Roughened with waves.

Far, to the edge of this world,
Stretches the golden illuminated
Sough brush;
So low on the horizon.

The horizon sky is gentled
With distant smooth clouds.
The sky is light.

A raven flies
From the shadows
Into the first sunlight.
His liquid wings
Turn silver.

I long to follow.

Northern Eskimo Verses

This poem comes from the »Trail Blazer,« July/August 1975. It was offered without title and signed Tina Willoya with no explanation about the poet. Willoya is a northern Eskimo name.

I SEE THE GENTLENESS

I see
The gentleness people are not afraid to show
Any more
The basic brother love being realized,
Emotions portrayed and hidden by those who look
And don't look.

I see.

I love
The feelings streaming into me and pouring out
Of me,
The look in the eyes of a person who feels
As I feel.

Aleut Prose

In the early 1970s jobs and educational opportunities drew many Alaska Natives to urban areas of the state and today Anchorage, the state's population center, is known as the »biggest Native village of them all« with over 10,000 Indians, Aleuts and Eskimos in residence.

For many the change from a lifestyle of subsistence hunting to urban living was rough. Aleut Phil Kelly was among the first to arrive, moving at age 15 with his family from the small fishing village of Egegik to Anchorage. Today a Native leader who commutes between Anchorage assignments and Egegik where he fishes in season, he remembers the move as traumatic. Acceptance was not quickly or easily won.

THE CITY

We come to the city
All dressed up and pretty
In clothes that we bought
That cost quite a lot…
Yet why are they laughing?
Almost in tears?
After all, these are clothes
Mail ordered from Sears…
We tried to be friendly
And be of good cheer,
Instead we are »Natives«
And it's said with a leer.

Athabascan Poetry

The following poem was printed under the name, Keefa the Rhymer, in the »Trail Blazer,« July/August 1975. This paper is put out by the Cook Inlet Native Association which is in the heart of Athabascan Indian country although many of its members are from other areas.

THE WINGS OF PERCEPTION

Unfold your wings, your Eagle wings,
The wings of your perception.
Fly where the air is clear
And see through your deception.

You have no limits, understand
The time has come to fly
Above the plains of misery
And walking in a lie.

Soar my brother, glide and laugh
Upon the highest peak.
Pride is where the air is clear;
Self pity makes you weak.

Trim your wings and see through hate
Perceive the self deception
That keeps you grounded, spread your wings!
The wings of your perception.

Post-War Tlingit

Turn-of-the century ethnographer John R. Swanton recorded many Tlingit songs but reported few of them made sense unless you understood their legends. This one was a favorite song when peace was made after a great war with a change of name for the lucky clan that escaped.

If you had died, Kagwantan's children
For you I would have cut off my hair
So much I love you.
For you I would have blackened my face,
Kagwantan's children.

Chilkatcanoe Love Song

In the late 1930s Carol Beery Davis of Juneau published a book of translations and music for Tlingit songs and a favorite of the collection was one on love and friendship.

Best peace together,
Taklewedi children.
You know this world will get dark
So we are to be in friendship.

Old Inupiat(-Eskimo) woman at Kotzebue, ice-fishing for a meal of arctic char and grayling for her family and relatives.

Seal hunter at Point Hope, one of the most traditional Inupiat(-Eskimo) villages in Alaska and ideally located at a point of land that juts out into the Chukchi Sea, where the bowhead whale passes close to the shore during its annual migration from the Bering Sea to the Arctic Ocean.

Hooper Bay, Yup'ik (-Eskimo) community along the Bering Sea coast, subsisting on fishing and game hunting, waits for the spring sun to thaw its icy fetters.

Walrus colony on Round Island close to Dillingham; the whiskered giants that roam the Bering Sea and other Alaskan waters are hunted by the Natives for their meat and their ivory for carving.

The humpback whale, as seen here in Southeastern coastal waters, is one of 15 species of large whales that inhabit Alaskan waters; while the Aleuts and Eskimos of the north have always relied on whale hunting as the mainstay of their villages' economy, the Indians of Southeastern Alaska have included them in their folk tales instead.

Spring break-up in
the tundra, near
Scammon Bay in the
Yukon Delta National
Wildlife Refuge.

▷

Sammy Sam, an
Athabascan Indian, in
front of his home.

Two Tlingit boys
enjoy the fun of
motorcycling.

Crest of a totem pole,
carved by Tlingit
Indians from yellow
cedar, in Ketchikan's
Totem Bight Park,
now a National
Historic Site.

Stampede of musk oxen on Nunivak Island in the Bering Sea; they are the last horned survivors from the Pleistocene Age.

Polar bear with cub on the ice of the Arctic Ocean near Wainwright.

Arctic fox in the tundra north of the Brooks Range.

Barrow, called "Top of the World," is the largest Eskimo community of Alaska and the northernmost settlement. It has become a focal point of Native-rights action and hosts the smallest college, the Inupiat University of the Arctic, right on the shores of the Arctic Ocean.

Midnight sun over the ice of the Arctic Ocean at Point Barrow.

Migrating sandhill
cranes in Denali
National Park.

Lone skier in the
Chugach Mountains.

RECREATION AND SPORTS IN ALASKA by Nancy Simmerman

Journal entry: Denali National Park, July 3.

Camping and hiking is not like it used to be in the Park. I remember when the grizzlies were properly timid – one glimpse of a back-country traveler sent the bruin running at top speed over the nearest ridge to the valley beyond. This summer the bears are everywhere – and agressive.

A few weeks before one nipped a retreating photographer in the backside. Last night a curious blond grizzly woke me at 4.00 A.M. by grunting and puffing on the fragile nylon wall of my tent. Today while hiking, I offered a bear my pack rather than me. Hoping the gift would stop his measured advance, I retreated up the side of treeless Cathedral Mountain. »Take my food, play with the feathers in my sleeping bag, jump on the cameras, but, please,« I pleaded silently, »don't find the exposed film.«

A wilderness photographer to the last – almost. I wasn't taking pictures of this bear.

The young grizzly sat down lazily on a mossy tundra hummock 50 yards from my pack. He observed my humble, perhaps frantic, efforts to convince him that I was not a succulent young caribou.

Watching me, he stretched out prone on his stomach, loose-jointed puppy-dog style, with his head on his paw. My waving arms and Indian whoops were most likely the strangest thing he'd encountered that day. Soon there was no movement from him. Through binoculars I could see that I'd bored him mightily and he'd given himself to the soft tundra cushion and the sun's warmth. He slept, 50 yards from my pack. Five hundred pounds of bear.

A few more minutes of quiet watching and I was sure I didn't want to be around when he awoke. With loudly beating heart and my eyes glued to his limp form, I retrieved my pack. The large aluminum frame pack, which had been an abominably heavy load 20 minutes earlier, now was unnoticed on my back as I half-ran down the swale. One doesn't run from a bear, I knew, even a sleeping bear. That's most likely why the aforementioned photographer was nipped in the rear.

En route, before reaching the Park road, I sighted three more grizzlies, this time a sow and two yearling cubs. A caribou grazed on the open tundra between us. The bears were coming my way. I knew the caribou could run faster than I.

Panting with relief, I reached the road and the shuttle bus arrived before the bears did. My outward calm covered a residual inner tension as I sank into the seat with a sigh.

Alaska, together with northern Canada, represents a last vast wilderness, complete with untraveled ridges, unpopulated river valleys and unexpected encounters with wildlife. Alaska also represents people. The settlements – Ketchikan, Juneau, Anchor Point, Talkeetna, Fairbanks, Allakaket, Barrow and, yes, even metropolitan Anchorage – viewed from the window of a high-flying jet plane are no more than pockets in the seemingly limitless wilderness.

From Anchorage's Taiga subdivision of luxury houses, walk 20 minutes eastward, spread out your sleeping bag and wait for the first visitor. Your chances are roughly 50-50 of seeing a bear or a moose before a human. This encounter could occur within the first day, the first week or not until the end of the first year of your encampment. You are within sound of city activity, yet the land is wild and mostly untraveled. Despite its designation as Chugach State Park, this land is not »Sunday afternoon picnic« country for the uninitiated.

Some of us gleefully search out the farthest reaches of the land, in summer treasuring the solitude, in winter sharing on skis the quiet and remoteness with a friend. Other Alaskans travel the narrow strips of pavement, touch the fringes with a picnic or short hike, then return to the »Stateside« comfort of an all-electric Anchorage home and nearby health club. A few hardy souls choose to spend 365 days a year in isolated log cabins, leading frugal lives of fishing, wood gathering and simple pleasures.

Wherever the location, many an Alaskan has chosen his or her particular address for a common reason: the quality of lifestyle and the diversity of recreation available. Alaskans like to be close to nature. They can retreat easily from the demands of urban life, either by driving a few minutes from the city or by changing lifestyle completely.

The composition of Alaska's population has shifted in the last 15 years. A survey of outdoor recreation activity, compiled in 1967 by the Alaska Department of Natural Resources from interviews with a statistical cross-section of Alaskans throughout the state, showed the average Alaskan to be strongly sports oriented, spending a large amount of available leisure time participating in outdoor sports ranging from berry picking and flying light planes to alpine skiing and tennis.

A similar survey completed in 1981 shows an overall decrease in the percent of the population participating in outdoor sports, although major increases have occured in a few sports: tennis, cross-country skiing, pleasure flying and four-wheel driving.

The dramatic population increase, concurrent with the construction of the Trans-Alaska oil pipeline, may have brought to Alaska a more urban-oriented person, one who came, with family, for the work rather than qualities found in Alaska itself. Many of our newcomers at first are not oriented toward outdoor sports and the unique qualities of Alaska experience. After a long winter or two, bouts with cabin fever and encouragement from sports-minded friends, cheechakos often discover that an active lifestyle benefits both the mind and the body.

The overall pace of life seems to have quickened as well in recent years. New regulations and restrictions are confusing. Paper work increases. Lines of people and automobiles become crowding.

»We are busier than we used to be,« complain longtime Alaskans, »and we have less time for sports and other recreation.«

To fill whatever time is available, a sports-oriented transplant from any city in the world will find familiar sports in Anchorage. Add to the urban facilities the availability of wilderness and water sports, then the sky is not even the limit.

Ballooning, sky diving, gliding, hang gliding, curling, bowling, raquetball, tennis, volleyball, basketball, baseball, softball, soccer, hockey, golf, karate, bicycling, dance, running, swimming, kayaking, canoeing, sailing, power boating, scuba diving, beach combing, water skiing, alpine skiing, hiking, rock climbing, mountaineering and ice fishing, all are within a short distance from Anchorage. Several sports which are well suited to the Alaska climate and terrain are especially popular: cross-country skiing, dog mushing, snowmobiling, four-wheel driving, flying light planes, fishing, hunting and camping.

The one sport cutting across cultural and geographical boundaries in Alaska is basketball. A ball, a hoop and a small flat area, indoors or out, are sufficient for a start. Most communities can supply this. Southeastern teen-agers shoot baskets in the rain; Yukon River kids lob the ball at −40°F. Kotzebue kids even play under the midnight sun.

But from the tundra game to an organized competition is a long step. Jim Mahaffey, long-time Alaska coach and outdoor education instructor at Alaska Pacific University, explained the problems of finding competition for teams in such a far-flung state. »Even if a village of 400 residents can develop a high school athletic program, can you imagine what it costs to fly two small airplanes from Savoonga to Koyuk? It's about $3,000 for one weekend.

»Anywhere in the bush, figure the transportation cost at about $300 for just one plane load. The nearest village with a team might be one hundred or more miles away, so you've got real money problems.«

One solution, Mahaffey went on to explain, is concurrent competition. The six-seat plane flies the boys' team from Village A to Village B. On the return flight to pick up the remainder of the boys, it flies a girls' team from Village B to Village A. A nice solution when it works. Dangerous flying conditions associated with severe cold and short arctic days can strain the nerves of the most relaxed parents.

But the bush villages aren't the only ones with difficulty in finding competition. The University of Alaska, Fairbanks, must travel 350 miles to Anchorage to find the only other collegiate competition in the state. Consequently both Anchorage and Fairbanks university teams make frequent and lengthy trips to competition Outside, a costly endeavor in money, student time and energy. For this reason only a few collegiate teams travel extensively, notably basketball, cross-country ski, men's hockey and women's volleyball. Several semi-professional baseball teams: the Fairbanks Gold Panners, the Anchorage Glacier Pilots, the Mat-Su Miners, Cook Inlet Bucs, North Pole Nicks, and the Peninsula Oilers face similar competition scarcity. An increasingly successful alternative for both collegiate and professional teams is to lure Outside teams north. There's now a major college basketball tournament each fall in Anchorage.

If basketball is the most popular sport across Alaska, cross-country skiing is trying for second place. Of all the households in southcentral Alaska, 38 percent have cross-country skis. A growing popularity in the bush is the result of a strong urban program.

High school and college cross-country ski programs provide a total experience for the competitors, from foot and roller ski races during pre-season conditioning to post-competition spring ski tours, hiking and camping trips. With large numbers of young people skiing, Alaskans have consistently placed well in national Nordic events. Each year since 1972, at least one Alaska young man or woman has earned a place on either the U.S. Olympic or the F.I.S. team. Six Alaskans went to the 1976 Olympics in Nordic events.

Nor is Alaskan cross-country skiing limited to students and young people. The Anchorage Nordic Ski Club registers 2,000 members, a Fairbanks club is proportionally strong and many more Alaskans ski without concern for affiliation.

Alaskans push other sports to illogical limits as well. Whether snowmobiling, skiing, running, rafting or dog mushing, if a race of stamina can be made from the sport, Alaskans will do it.

Typical is the Mt. Marathon foot race held in the seaport town of Seward each July Fourth, Independence Day. It traces its history to two gold miners' bar room bet. The runners climb 2,900 vertical feet up a grueling mountain trail to the check point, then return to finish at the base of the mountain. Part of the descent is a wild slide down a snowfield; part consists of bruising leaps down rocky cliffs. Winning time: about 44 minutes.

Another demanding race, both of dogs and men, is the March Iditarod Dog Sled Race, starting near

Anchorage and finishing more than 1,000 miles away in Nome. Many participants quit the race long before Nome, victims of exhaustion, severe cold weather or failed equipment.

In the tradition of the historic 1925 sled race against time to bring diphtheria serum to Nome, the competition captures more of the heroism, the color and the mystique of Alaska than any other northern sporting event.

Competition is tough. In 1978, after 15 days of sledding and camping in bitter cold weather, incredibly, Dick Mackey of Wasilla crossed the Nome finish line one second before defending champion Rick Swenson of Eureka to claim the $12,000 prize. In addition, almost every winter weekend finds dogteams racing in several towns around the state.

To look at sports in Alaska, we must necessarily differentiate between urban Alaskans and bush Alaskans. Urban Alaska consists of the major communities: Anchorage, Juneau, Fairbanks, Kenai, Wrangell and the like. The bush can range from the lone homsteader to small villages isolated from the mainstream of Alaska life by physical barriers of water, forest or tundra. Location greatly determines lifestyle and recreational opportunities.

Both urban and bush residents may hunt, fish, pick berries, travel on snowmobiles and snowshoes, run boats, gather firewood, walk and ski, but generally their reasons for doing so are vastly different. While the resident of Shageluk is performing chores necessary to survival, the Fairbanks resident, after work, has many options open, from a workout at the gym to bowling in a league. Or he may choose to snowshoe untracked hillsides on a Sunday afternoon, navigating the Tanana River or realizing the pleasure of serving self-caught fish. Hardly necessary to survival in Fairbanks, the activities provide a change of pace for the mind and a necessary physical release for the body.

Wherever the bush Alaskan might live, from the islands of Southeastern to the Arctic coast, daily routine is never routine. A subsistence lifestyle consists almost entirely of seasonal activities: fishing, hunting, boating, dog mushing, snowmobiling, cabin building, all of which can become recreation when shared with friends. Berry picking and fish camp are eagerly anticipated social events for Eskimo and Indian families. Muscles harden with daily chores, craft work is both utilitarian and beautiful, leisure time is rare.

Whereas in the past the hunting-fishing-gathering cultures provided strongly physical daily activities for the entire family, today's village-centered societies revolve around the general store, the mail-order catalog, church, school and each other. Highly social people live in the bush, but they generally like humanity in small doses. A favorite recreational activity among adults is »visiting.« It reinforces friendships, builds a sense of community and provides a chance to talk shop: »How's that new wind generator working?« »My snowgo fell through the ice yesterday.« »When you go to Kotzebue, could you look for red yarn to match this?«

Few adults in the bush make time to participate in organized competitive sports, although a resurgence of dog mushing events has occured recently. The popularity of the Iditarod races has turned many people from snowmobiles back toward the traditional dog-powered sleds.

Until recently, facilities have not been available to encourage indoor sports. Teen-agers and young adults especially, during the long winters, need outlets for excess creative and physical energy. The State of Alaska is attempting to build high schools in all villages requesting them. With high school facilities often comes a gymnasium. I talked about the effect of the new Ambler gym with Anore Jones, since 1967 a resident of this Kobuk River community of less than 200 people.

»The gym gives us our first indoor place to play, so important when winter is cold and dark. There's not much else for kids to do during the Christmas holidays and after school.

»Having facilities for basketball has actually helped both young and old, because if we don't have a school tournament scheduled with other villages, then different Ambler teams play each other. I play with the Mama Bears, the ladies. Keith, my husband, plays with the city league or the Papa Bears, and sometimes they play against the high school girls. Or we mix and match and make up teams and anybody can play. You can know nothing about basketball and still have a fine time. A lot of people play; a lot of people watch.

»Basketball fits in really well with the lifestyle up here where everyone lives in small houses with large families, a lot of noise and body contact. Basketball has that closeness with its noise, excitement and physical contact.

»We're just beginning to introduce cross-country skiing, which is a perfect complement to basketball. Skiing talks to the other side of bush life which is outdoor and solitary. Hunting, trapping and traveling are as much a part of our life as the gregarious close-packed living quarters.

»Keith, who competed in skiing 20 years ago in Fairbanks, began last year to coach a cross-country ski/ biathlon program similar to the one John Miles has in western Alaska. Skiing is new to the Eskimos, but with rifle shooting, there's a strong tie with the culture. Some of the boys now like to go rabbit hunting on skis.

»The pace of life has been increasing very fast as we become more modernized and get electricity and plumbing. The growth of competitive sports in Ambler seems to be part of the change.«

The biathlon program in western Alaska Anore mentioned was begun in 1977 by John Miles, a teacher at Koyuk on the Bering Sea. In an effort to counteract the problems of boredom and lack of challenge found by so many young people in bush villages, Miles, consulting with Jim Mahaffey, has developed a program pulling together skills and facilities which abound in almost every northern community: snow, rifles and wilderness. By adding cross-country skis and a coach, a biathlon team emerges. The biathlon, an event in the Olympic games, requires the competitor to ski a prepared trail, carrying his rifle. At designated stops along the trail, the skier must shoot at targets from specified distances and body positions. A missed target adds to the skier's elapsed time. Both swift skiing and a steady shooting arm are required. At this writing, Alaska is the only state in the U.S.A. to offer a biathlon program in elementary schools – and this in the far reaches of the Arctic!

Traditionally in Native communities, women have not taken part in sporting activities. For basketball and skiing, no tradition exists and an enthusiastic group of girls now competes. It seems safe to predict that one day an Alaska Eskimo or Indian boy or girl will compete on the U.S. Olympic cross-country or biathlon ski team.

Beyond Anchorage and Fairbanks, beyond the villages, lie yet another recreational Alaska – the far wilderness, the land between the villages. Entrance is by plane, foot, boat or skis from the nearest habitation. The appearance of the land is no different from that which lies closer to the towns, but the traveler feels the difference.

One summer a Swiss city couple joined me for a wilderness trip in the Brooks Range. Sitting near our lakeside pile of packs, food and kayaks, we experienced a heady freedom as the bush plane, which brought us here, disappeared into the distance. We would be picked up three weeks from this day on a gravel bar 350 miles downriver.

Before making camp, I lectured them on the ways of the wilderness.

»We take no chances. No one will look for us before the pickup date, so we must not create an emergency.«

I told them how to avoid bears and what to do in the unlikely event of an attack. I told them how to live with great clouds of mosquitoes. My visitors enjoyed the »game.«

Several days later one of the visitors had a slight mishap. A flipped kayak and a few wet clothes, nothing more. But now they saw this was not a game. There was no road over the next ridge. No help would appear whatever happened. By choice we carried no radio. We were here to meet nature on her terms. Their panic drove them to irrational decisions.

»We must begin now to walk for help!«

»Why do we need help?« I asked. »We have food, tents, kayaks, everything, and no injuries. To reach a village would be many weeks of hard walking over mountains – if we could cross the rivers. And if we become lost or injured, the pilot would not know where to look for us. No, we must stay on our route.«

»But perhaps we cannot reach the pickup place in time. No one will look for us, and it is absolutely necessary that we be back in Switzerland to return to our jobs on time.«

»The pilot will not forget us. That is not the Alaskan way. If we are not at the pickup place, he will fly up the river until he finds us. He may not be able to land, but he will learn if we need help or only more time.«

»But suppose we should need a doctor! We might die before help could come!«

So, my Swiss visitors learned the way of the wilderness, and most of Alaska is wilderness.

In Alaska the individual is an integral part of the flow of the land and the flow of the water, must live by nature's laws, and must abide by the results of decisions. If a decision is poor, the wilderness might permit a second chance. Perhaps not.

When a person is an integral part of the flow of the land and the water and moves with the rhythm of the land, there is no finer experience on earth.

We know a feeling of almost unlimited space, of nature, untamed, unpredictable and with dazzling beauty. Some are frightened by the lack of urban security beyond the city limits. Others find meaning, excitement and a personal challenge. The dichotomy of civilization superimposed upon wilderness has created a special breed of people, in love with the land, the sea and the active life.

THE OUTDOORSMAN'S ALASKA by Jim Rearden

The frosty dawn of September 1, 1982, opening day of Alaska's moose season, found me in the Caribou Hills of the Kenai Peninsula with an Indian friend, Walter Johnson. For a quarter of a century I have hunted moose annually in this area, and I have fed my family largely on moose meat I have killed on those hunts.

We silently walked toward a hillside where we could watch a 500-yard-diameter clearing amid the spire-topped spruce forest. The previous evening we had silently searched several clearings for moose and moose sign. We saw no moose, but in this particular muskeggy, low willow and grass-covered clearing we had found fresh tracks and still-soft, dark, droppings. Several moose had fed there recently. About 15 years earlier I killed a three-year-old bull moose in that clearing, and I knew it was still a favorite haunt of these great animals.

As we left our tent the frosty ground crunched if we stepped wrongly, so we moved slowly, picking each step, determined that if moose were in the clearing we wouldn't alert them.

We reached the hillside where we could see across the clearing. Morning fog rose from nearby gin-clear Deep Creek, and from tiny ponds in the clearing. I kept my hands in my pockets for warmth, and had my binoculars tucked inside my shirt so they wouldn't fog when I used them. All was silent. There were no moose in the clearing.

Walter watched one area, and I walked about 50 feet away so I could see another. The sky lightened as the sun rose over the distant glacier-hung mountains.

After a time I saw movement at the edge of the clearing and focused the binoculars there. A cow moose, her dark brown and black body contrasting sharply with the yellowed dead grass, stepped into view to stand staring over the clearing, big ears up, alert. She stood motionless for several minutes. I tossed a small rock to get Walter's attention, and he quietly joined me, peering through his binoculars at the cow.

Finally satisfied, the cow stepped from the thick brush and into the opening, and started to feed. Another moose suddenly appeared 20 feet behind her, and even without binoculars we could see its three-foot-spread antlers, small from a trophy hunter's standpoint, but perfect for a meat animal. The distance was about 300 yards, and it was clear we would have to shoot from where we were: the bull could be out of sight in a few steps if we alerted him while trying to move closer.

As we readied our rifles a third moose appeared in the same area. It was a bull, almost a twin to the first. »You take the bull on the right, I'll take the other,« I suggested quietly. Walter nodded, eyes crinkling with a smile above his high brown cheekbones, and we both aimed. As Walter's rifle roared I touched my trigger, holding sights on the deepest part of my animal, aiming for a lung or a heart shot. We had to shoot offhand, for there were no nearby trees to rest against. The hillside sloped steeply in front of us, and we could see the moose only through a small window in the trees.

At the roar of the two rifles both bulls stumbled a few steps, and stood, heads down. The cow ran a short way, turned, and rejoined the bulls. There she milled about, frightened. Walter's bull slowly collapsed; moments later my bull dropped.

Our planned week-long moose hunt had lasted about 45 minutes, and we were slightly disappointed. The fun is over when the game is bagged. But our families would eat well during the coming winter with moosemeat in our home freezers.

Annually 10,000 or more Alaskan moose – the world's largest deer – are killed mostly by meat hunters. However, because of the six-foot or greater spread antlers carried by some Alaskan moose, trophy hunters from around the world travel to Alaska to hunt them, as well as other big game.

Only adjacent Canada can compare with Alaska's offering of ivory-clawed, hump-shouldered grizzly bears, the blazing white golden-horned Dall sheep, white-necked huge-antlered caribou, spike-horned mountain goats, and others. Alaska has the largest number of species of big game of any of the 50 states of the United States.

Many residents came to Alaska because of its wildness, its freedoms, its beauty, and for the grand hunting and fishing it offers.

While I have hunted most of Alaska's big game species, mostly for meat, I appreciate the grandeur of a great trophy, and I've taken trophy-class Dall sheep, caribou, mountain goat, grizzly and black bear, as well as moose. When I was a registered guide some of my clients took fine trophies. Knowing the habits of the game helped tremendously when seeking trophies for clients who wanted the biggest and best. I once guided a brewery owner from an eastern state who wanted a great caribou bull for his trophy room. I chartered the plane of a bush pilot and had him fly us into the Twin Lakes country at the base of the Alaska Peninsula, where the Mulchatna caribou herd lives.

Caribou travel forever, in endless circles and migrations, feeding and resting as they go. In the fall they trek north past the small lake where we camped. No man can catch a traveling caribou, but if you can see a caribou coming, you can often head him off. We hunted by sitting quietly on a hillside and studying the land with binoculars, watching for the telltale glint of golden antlers in the sun, or the flash of the white neck of an old bull.

In three days only one band of six cows and calves nervously traveled through. One day we watched a great bow-legged, straw-colored grizzly bear sow with twin cubs as they fed on berries. The scuffling, pestiferous cubs drove the mother wild, and about once an hour she would slap one of them on the rear hard enough for us to hear it bawl from the hundreds of yards away.

Philip, my hunter, was polite, but unimpressed by the caribou hunting. He clearly thought we were wasting our time. On the fourth day he asked if we could delay going to our lookout point until afternoon: he wanted to cast for lake trout near camp. At midmorning, with Philip catching and releasing two-foot-long lake trout along the beach by our tent, and while I was re-salting a cape from a Dall ram we had taken earlier, I saw five white-necked caribou bulls single-filing into a gulley a mile or more away, at the end of the lake.

»Caribou,« I called to Philip and snatched the binoculars and ran to our folding boat. Philip grabbed his rifle and we ran the little outboard motor at full speed the length of the lake, and I rammed the boat up on the beach and beckoned to Philip to follow me, fast, the 400 yards to a willow draw.

»They went *that* way,« he protested, pointing, and trying to stop me. He was right, but there wasn't time to explain. I shook my head and urged him on. »In the willows« he repeated, looking at me as if I had gone crazy.

I had no time to explain. Just then the five bulls came into sight about 300 yards away, walking directly toward us. I grinned, and Philip looked amazed. »How did you know they would come this way?« he demanded, whispering as he readied his rifle.

The rest was easy. Philip had two caribou tags and he was a good shot. When the five bulls were within easy range I pointed out the one with the finest and largest antlers and he dropped it in its tracks. As the others turned, confused by the shot, I pointed out the second largest, and when the shooting was done the two bulls lay dead 50 feet apart, and Philip had two magnificent trophies for his wall. Also, my family ate the meat of those caribou that winter.

How had I known that the bulls would turn 90 degrees and travel directly toward us?

I hadn't known for sure, but I had a good idea. Three days earlier from our lookout stand I had watched the band of six cows and calves walk through the draw that the five bulls had walked into – and the cows had made an abrupt turn and had filed straight to the willow draw where I had hustled Philip.

Although it had been days since the cows and calves had followed that route, I knew the bulls would probably follow the same course, in fact I gambled on it. This is one of the few predictable actions of caribou that I know. I have seen a band of single-filing caribou weave across a ridge, travel down a slope, wade a river, and climb another ridge to disappear within an hour. A day or two later I have watched another band follow the identical route of the first, including seemingly illogical and abrupt changes in direction.

Until recently virtually all of Alaska's 375 million acres (except for several national parks) were open to hunting. This has changed greatly since the 1971 Congressional action to grant to Alaska's Eskimos, Aleuts and Indians 44 million acres of land. Appended to the law that did this was a small section that called for Congress to set aside up to 80 million acres of national interest lands for wildlife refuges, national wild and scenic rivers, national forest and national parks.

By December, 1980, when Congress acted, the 80 million acres had grown to 104 million acres. Most Alaskans regard the law as an anti-hunting act, for it has stopped sport hunting in 13 new or expanded national parks (the act *doubled* the area covered by U.S. national parks).

Although the new national parks are closed to sport hunting, subsistence hunting in them by rural Alaskans will be permitted, and the law establishes subsistence use as a priority use of fish and game on *all* federal lands in Alaska, or about 65 percent of the state.

Anywhere from about 15 percent to as high as 50 percent of the harvest of various species of big game will be lost because of the closure of these lands to sport hunting. The full impact of this law will be years in making itself felt.

Thus trophy hunters coming to Alaska, or those living in Alaska, must plan carefully where they hunt. It is likely that all of the land granted to Alaska's Natives will be closed to the public for hunting, and this includes some of the state's best hunting land. The newly established parks, especially the Wrangell-Saint Elias National Park, a huge extension of the Alaska Range with the Denali National Park, and two vast parks and preserves in the center of the Brooks Range, remove sport hunting from about 27 million acres of the finest hunting lands in Alaska. Alaska's growing rural villages where live mostly Eskimos and Indians, are exerting increasing pressure on fish and game, for many of the villagers depend upon wild foods for their existence. The wise sportsman seeking big game in Alaska avoids hunting near these villages, expecially for moose and caribou, the primary food animals of rural Alaska. These villages are mostly along main rivers, such as the Yukon, Tanana, Koyukuk, and Kuskokwim. The delta of the Yukon and Kuskokwim Rivers, for example, supports about 55 Eskimo villages and

18,000 people. Most of these people depend heavily upon fish and game for their basic food.

But there are plenty of remote, mountainous game lands left, where the only practical way to get there is by small plane, and where few if any Alaskans live year-round. Alaska's guides, who are assigned areas in which they may take clients hunting, know these areas, and the wise visitor carefully selects a guide of good repute, and depends upon him to find the desired trophy or trophies. Nowadays Alaska big game hunts emphasize quality, not quantity, of game. The time of the two-week hunt in which three or four species of big game were bagged, is gone forever in Alaska.

With less land to hunt and more hunters, many species and areas of Alaska are now hunted only by permit. Details on permit hunts are available usually by July preceding the fall hunting season from the Alaska Department of Fish and Game, Subport Building, Juneau, Alaska 99801.

There are some bright spots. That trophy of trophies, the great Alaska brown/grizzly bear (one highly variable species, found over much of the state) is as abundant today as it has been in perhaps half a century. These bears are unpredictable and dangerous, and annually about 50 of them are killed by Alaskans defending their lives or their property. No one should venture into brown/grizzly country without a rifle capable of stopping the charge of one of these huge (up to 1,500 pounds) animals. Most bears flee at the sight, sound, and smell of man, but enough don't so that carrying a bear rifle is a way of life in much of Alaska.

Sportsmen, who are limited to one brown bear every four years, bag 800 to 900 of these big bears annually, and slightly more than half of these are killed by non-residents, who, in order to hunt these animals, must have a guide. Top bear producing country is probably the Alaska Peninsula, where an annual average kill of about 150 is made. Kodiak and Afognak Islands are next-most-popular for big bear hunts. The average bear killed on these islands carries a hide that squares (average of greatest width and greatest length) about seven and a half feet, but an occasional nine-footer is still taken.

The Admiralty, Baranof, and Chichagof Islands of northern southeastern Alaska, the rain forest Panhandle, produce the next largest number of brown/grizzlies. These are dark-colored animals, and they are hunted morning and evening on coastal tidal flats, and along salmon spawning streams.

Dall sheep are plentiful in Alaska, with a total population of about 50,000 animals. Annually in recent years sportsmen have killed about 1,200 rams (rams only, with 7/8 curl horns may be killed). The establishment of the new national parks reduces by about half the number of rams available to sport hunters, so the kill of rams can be expected to decrease to perhaps 500 or 600 animals annually.

Non-residents must also have a guide to hunt the Dall sheep, and around 70 percent of the guided non-residents have been successful in taking trophies. Best hunting had been where the new national parks have been established – in the Wrangell Mountains, in the central Alaska Range, and in the Brooks Range. Alaska's sheep hunters are now seeking formerly unhunted areas for sheep.

Wolves are classified as big game in Alaska, and there may be between 10,000 and 15,000 of these huge (up to 135 pounds for a male) predators living in Alaska. The wolf is the most wary of all Alaskan mammals, and is a trophy of opportunity: the fortunate hunter who encounters a wolf usually does so while hunting other species.

The bumbling but often wary black bear is common in most of Alaska's subarctic and the seasons for these great game animals have traditionally been long, with generous (up to three annually) bag limits. Best hunting for black bears is probably in Prince William Sound, on the Gulf of Alaska, and along some of the salmon spawning streams of the southeastern Alaska Panhandle, and on the Kenai Peninsula. Black bear hunters also do well in above-timberline areas of the Alaska Range.

Moose are widespread, but scarce near areas of high human population. Some areas of the state are managed for trophy moose, and hunters interested must participate in a drawing. There are still many remote areas, however, where trophy moose are abundant. Caribou herds are found generally throughout mainland Alaska, and on the Alaska Peninsula, with roughly 13 identifiable herds, numbering perhaps half a million animals in all. Largest herd is the 100,000 Porcupine caribou herd, named for the stream it often lives near; it spends part of the year in the high arctic of northeastern Alaska, and part of the year in the Yukon Territory.

Mountain goats, which are really more closely allied to antelopes than goats, are found mostly in the mountains of coastal Alaska. They have been hunted rather heavily in recent years, and goat hunting throughout the state is now by permit.

Alaska is developing, and her human population has leaped by a quarter in the past decade, largely due to development. New land legislation has put a lot of new lines on maps. But get into a small airplane and fly over this great wild land. Those map lines don't show: you'll see occasional trails, and few highways and towns.

Quality is also the word for Alaska's sport fishing. Unlike big game hunting, sport fishing has largely been unaffected by the establishment of new parks, refuges, and Native-owned lands.

Consider: Alaska has 34,000 miles of coastline, including islands as well as deep-inlets of clear green water, backed by steep-sided conifer-covered mountains. There are huge bays, and small; islands, and islets. There are more than three million lakes, ranging from ponds you can almost toss a rock across, to 80-mile-long Lake Iliamna, Alaska's largest. Most of these lakes hold fish.

Salmon is what Alaska is all about. It has been the mainstay of life for centuries: villages became established where salmon can be caught annually, as they return on their strange and wonderful spawning runs. Salmon have brought more wealth to Alaska than gold. Five species of salmon live in Alaska's water. There are more than 2,000 major rivers where salmon spawn, not counting small streams and tributaries. In recent years commercial fishermen have taken as many as 100 million salmon in one season. No man can visualize that many fish. The numbers taken by sportsmen, by comparison, are insignificant.

What is it like to catch a really big salmon? I remember one. The deep-green water, clear for many feet down, was glassy. Snow-capped mountains rose steeply from the rocky beach, their lower slopes green with trees. Gulls quarreled nearby. A swimming seal's head left a wake on the placid surface as he swam past. As my small boat drifted I hooked a herring bait so it would spin as I retrieved. I cast and slowly brought it back, and cast again.

This time as I peered into the clear water to watch the bait struggle into sight a great silver-sided salmon flashed from the depths and seized it. The rod was almost jerked from my hands. The reel screamed, and I heaved back to set the hook – which was probably already set from the violence of the salmon's strike. The salmon leaped free of the water, my line hissing behind him, and he landed splat, flat on his side, tossing water in all directions. He leaped again, and walked on his tail, then went deep, and it felt as if I had hooked the seal that had just eased by. This was a king salmon, 58 pounds of red muscle sheathed in silver, a torpedo with gills, a great brute of a fish. Alaskans love this fish so much it is the official state fish.

I was fishing near Wrangell in southeastern Alaska (the Panhandle) and that big king fought my 25-pound test line and my limber pole until my shoulders ached and my wrists were tired.

He leaped and he dived and he towed my skiff. When he saw the skiff once, he screamed off about 200 yards of line in one tremendous run. I was afraid to tighten the drag on my reel more, and bare metal was beginning to show under my line when the king burned himself out, and I started to retrieve line.

That fish gave me such a fantastic fight, and I was so filled with admiration for him, that I almost released him when he wearily allowed me to pump him near and scoop a big net under his tired body. But the rich red flesh of king salmon is a gourmet's delight, and I kept him to eat and to share with friends.

He wasn't really a big king: I've seen 80-pounders. State record is currently 93 pounds caught by a sportsman. Commercially caught kings have reached 120 pounds and more.

The Alaska Panhandle, that southern, narrow strip, is 125 by 400 miles of sheltered inside waters dotted with hundreds of forest-covered islands, backed by glaciers and snow-capped peaks. It offers some of the finest saltwater salmon fishing anywhere – and all salmon are at their peak size, strength, and beauty, while they are still in salt water. Once they reach freshwater streams, headed for spawning grounds, they stop eating and live off stored fats in their bodies. Their silvery sides darken, and they lose weight to eventually become grotesque caricatures of themselves.

Charter boats are available in most southern coastal Alaska towns, and king salmon fishing is best in June and July, but some may be caught through August. Some fishermen rate the much smaller (average weight about ten pounds) silver or coho salmon right along with the great king. Silvers arrive on the heels of the kings, peaking in August in most areas, and there are about twice as many silvers as kings. Some purists have found they can catch silvers on streamers flies, and they use fine flyrods in their sport, both in salt water and fresh. Look for the stout silver salmon anywhere from the Panhandle to the Seward Peninsula, on the Bering Sea coast – the same area where the great king salmon ranges.

Next look for the pink salmon, or the humpback. He's the smallest salmon, averaging three to four pounds, with a maximum weight of slightly above ten pounds. He comes in swarms in some years, and the peak of the pink salmon migration throughout most Alaska waters is in July. These little fish hit spinners, spoons, and wobblers, and when fresh from the sea, give the fisherman with light tackle a fine fight.

Pink salmon like to travel in schools, following beaches into inlets and bays, until they reach their home spawning stream, then they may mill about where the fresh and saltwater mix. They'll sometimes blacken the water with their numbers, and individual fish continually leap clear, splashing as they fall back. »Getting rid of sea lice,« some fishermen claim. »Softening their eggs,« others say. No one really knows why salmon leap so much while en route to spawning areas. It may be sheer exuberance.

There's a place in Alaska that I call »The Great Arc of

Fishes.« This is the Bristol Bay region, which curves in a 150-mile arc north from the base of the Alaska Peninsula. Here are some of the cleanest, sweetest, clearest streams and lakes in the world, flowing over gravel spawning beds that seem just made for salmon. Red or sockeye salmon dominate these lakes and streams: in 1980 alone, more than 50 million of these ruby-fleshed, lovely, long-swimmers returned to spawn in lakes and streams of Bristol Bay. When young red salmon hatch they live for two or three years in the lakes and streams before descending to the sea where they mature and return to spawn in the streams and lakes of their birth. Hordes of rainbow trout, Dolly Varden, arctic char, lake trout, and even pike, grow fat on the millions and millions of red salmon fry and smolt produced by the Bristol Bay drainages.

As result, fishing in my Great Arc of Fishes is perhaps the finest in the world. Land your float plane on a lake and taxi to where a stream flows into it. Toss your fly, your spoon, your spinner, into the racing waters, and take your chances – for you never know what you'll catch. If it is summer or fall it might be a silver, a pink, or a king salmon. Or it might be a great two-foot-long, pink-spotted, green-backed Dolly Varden, one of Alaska's finest sport fishes. Or it might be a powerful black-spotted, red-striped rainbow trout, weighing more than 15 pounds.

Or it might be a grayling.

Grayling is a special fish, a creature of the North, with the Aurora Borealis flickering on its sides. And, like the lovely Aurora, the colors are subtle, shifting, and when you most want to see them, they're gone. A dead grayling has lost its colors, and is a dull gray or even black. But hook a grayling, bring it to the surface in the clear water where it lives, and allow it to lie on its side in the sunlight. You'll see the pinks, blues, and subtle reds of the Aurora. Yank it from the water and try to get those colors in a photograph, and you'll fail every time: they disappear when the fish leaves its watery home.

The arctic grayling is a country boy with manners. He is a gentleman. He is a dry fly fisherman's joy, and a spin-fisherman's delight. He'll happily hit a red cranberry on a tiny hook, or a small chunk of red flannel underwear. He'll leap out of the water and take a lightly floating dry fly on his way down. I've caught grayling on a bare shiny hook.

Catch a grayling and if he is 15 inches long (the largest grayling are around 23 or 24 inches), cast again, and you'll catch his twin. And again, another twin. Grayling of a size seem to travel together. The great flag-like dorsal fin of the arctic grayling separates him from all other northern fish: no other northern fish has anything like it. And, while in the water, that fin can be as colorful as any flag that ever waved.

Grayling are found commonly throughout most of Alaska in cool clear streams and lakes. He is the dandy fish of Alaska. He is a delicate, lovely creature that seems to become whatever a fisherman wants to make of him.

Besides all of that, the grayling's white flesh is delicious eating.

I have just touched the surface of the sportsman's Alaska. There are great jagged glacier-hung mountains and valleys beyond mountains and valleys. There are great forests, and vast treeless tundra plains that seem to stretch forever. A wide variety of wildlife is found here – nearly 80 species of mammals, including the strange arctic lemming, bats, and whales – and perhaps half that number in varieties of fish.

Although there is oil development going on, and increasing numbers of people, when you climb into a bush plane or charterboat you can be in wilderness that conceals bears or moose within a few miles of any city in the state. You can walk for half an hour up almost any river that crosses one of the few highways and find few signs of man, and plenty of sport fish. With the right guide you can find whatever it is you seek – wilderness solitude, exciting stalks for great big game trophies, or simply a great experience.

And you can enjoy beauty, for Alaska remains largely unchanged by the hand of man.

Bull moose in the
September taiga of
the Savage River area
of the Denali National
Park. Grizzly bears
can be frequently
observed in the same
parkland and
elsewhere in the
interior of Alaska and
in the Yukon
Territory.

Log cabin in Eagle,
northern terminus of
the Taylor Highway
and located on the
south bank of the
Yukon River,
bordering the Yukon-

Charley Rivers
National Preserve. In
the gold rush days,
Eagle was the main
port of entry from
Canada, and many
claims were staked in
the vicinity.

Urban Rahoi, hunter
and guide in the
Alaska Range.

The Arrigetch Peaks in the Brooks Range's Gates of the Arctic National Park with its many wild and scenic rivers, such as the Kobuk and Alatna, which provide outstanding wilderness rafting, canoeing and kayaking.

Alaska's millions of
lakes and thousands
of streams and rivers
and their abundance
of fish offer unlimited
opportunities to the
angler; smiling here
over a catch of king
salmon of close to 80
pounds.

Mountain climber's exultation on one of the peaks of the Alaska Range.

Tenting at Wonder Lake campground with Mt. McKinley.

Ice-climbing, here inside an ice cave on Glacier Bay, is becoming increasingly attractive for the courageous nature lover.

THE YUKON

Area: 186,000
square miles
Population: 25,000
Territory capital:
Whitehorse
Tallest mountain:
Mt. Logan,
19,850 feet

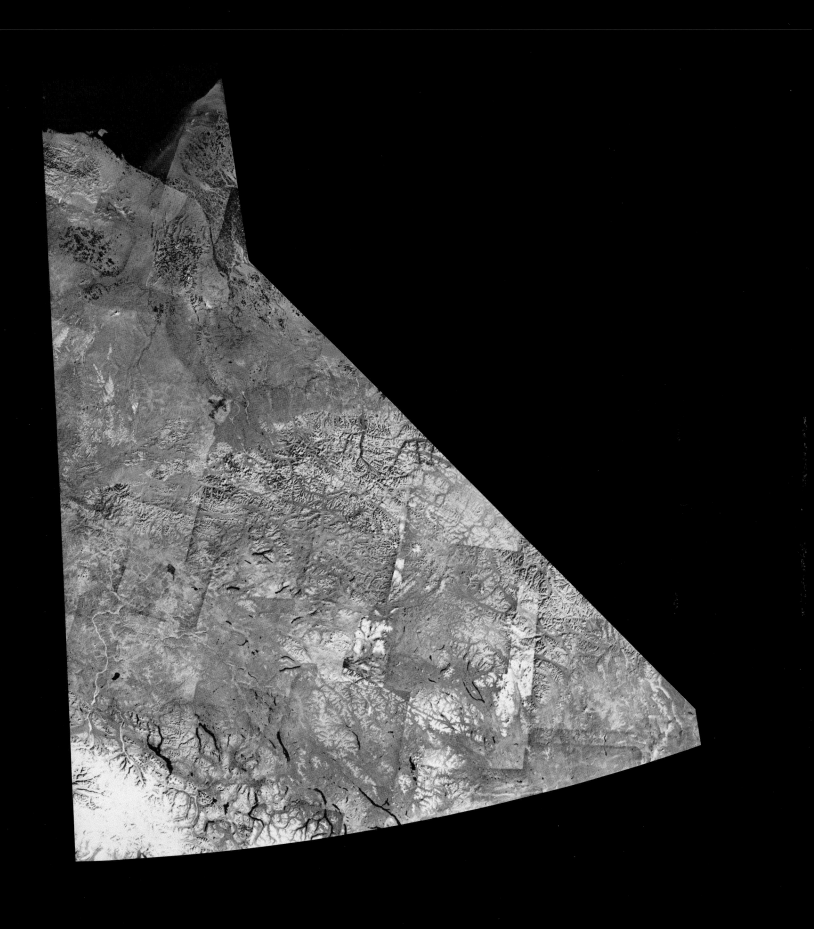

THE YUKON HISTORY by Dick North

A collage of mental imprints, some well-known, others less so, constitutes an area's history. As such, retrospection is more than a list of »important« events. It is a proliferation of ingredients, which when amalgamated, make up a region's character. Geographical considerations often mold this, particularly in tracts such as the Yukon Territory, where the climate, wilderness, and remote location combine to create a certain way of life. The object of this essay, therefore, is not to present a formal history, but, through anecdotes, to give the reader a »gut« feeling for the country and the people who live in it.

A family of prehistoric Indians trapped the dreaded *Felix atrox* (lion) in a pit on Old Crow Flats and destroyed the animal by hurling stones at it. Other species no longer living in the north, or extinct like the lion, were the wooly mammoth, great North American short-faced bear, stag-moose, yak, camel, American mastodon, saber-toothed cat, horse, badger, Saiga antelope, large-horned bison, and the ground sloth. Today, remains of these animals are constantly being dug up in gold placer operations.

Metis Andrey Glazunov mushed his dogs away from the safety of the Russian settlement at St. Michael's, Alaska in 1835 to cross to the Anvik River by way of an Eskimo portage. He followed the river to its mouth where it empties into an even bigger river which Glazunov called the Kwikpak, but other natives call the Yuk-khane. Both mean great river. The latter word stuck.

Hudson's Bay Company explorer Robert Campbell pushed his way through a huge encampment of Indians to meet the great chief of the coastal Tlingit tribes, Shakes, near the Stikine River, and thereby became the first white man to travel from the east via northern Canada to make contact with the coastal Indians. From the years 1839 through 1852 Campbell built a series of trading posts in what is now the Yukon Territory. First put up was Glenlyon House on Frances Lake; then a post at Pelly Banks where two Hudson's Bay Company men, Frobisher and Dubois, were to starve to death in 1850. Still later, Fort Selkirk was erected on the Yukon River. In 1852 this was plundered and destroyed by the fierce Chilkat Indians, who considered the interior their own trading area. Campbell gave up the fort and quit the country. The Chilkats returned to their village at Klukwan where they continued to reign supreme until the »white tide« overwhelmed them in the Klondike gold rush 46 years later.

Another Hudson's Bay Company man, John Bell, hauled the company's boats up the Rat River, a tributary of the Peel. He crossed a portage to the Porcupine River and drifted down it to the Yukon where he constructed Fort Yukon in 1847.

Twenty years later a new nation entered the northern scene when the United States purchased Alaska from Russia for the paltry sum of $7.2 million. This forced the Hudson's Bay Company to move their post from Fort Yukon up the Porcupine to an alternative site they named Rampart House.

W.H. Dall spent the years 1865-1868 working in Alaska and the Yukon for the Overland Telegraph Company. Dall's employment resulted from a scheme to build a telegraph line from the United States to Europe by way of the Bering Sea and Siberia. Stretches of the line actually were built in the Canadian north, but the entire project collapsed, when the first trans-Atlantic cable was laid in 1866. Dall's studies did much to acquaint the outside world with the northern interior. His partner, artist Fred Whymper, made the first published reference to the presence of gold in the Yukon valley in a book that came out in 1869.

Two footloose prospectors were floating down the Mackenzie River with their boat attached to a tree stump. Their one dream was of finding gold in the far-off Yukon River valley. They crossed the Rat River portage and joined up with a third partner in the Yukon basin. The three, Arthur Harper, Jack McQuesten and Albert Mayo, built a trading post they named Fort Reliance. It was only six miles down the Yukon River from the mouth of the Klondike River, but it took a little over two decades before the giant gold strike was made in the trio's own »backyard.« However, through providing a facility, they had laid the groundwork for the prospectors who were to come.

In the year 1882, the Yukon's first steamboat bucked the swift current as she headed upstream under command of her owner, Edward L. Scheiffelin. The testy little craft, the *New Racket* served her master well, but disgusted with the extremes of the country, Scheiffelin returned to the land where he had better pickings, Arizona. There, he made millions in the Tombstone silver mines. First, however, he sold his craft to McQuesten and his partners. They promptly renamed her the *Yukon*. Not only did they use her for travel, they also utilized the craft's pumping capacity to supply water to sluice sandbars for gold.

A white man stood atop Chilkoot Pass for the first time in 1875. His name was George Holt, who some-

110

how managed to elude the warlike Chilkat Indians that jealously guarded this gateway to the interior. He crossed the pass and descended as far as the headwaters of the Yukon and Teslin Rivers, and then returned the way he came to his point of origin, Sitka, capital of the territory of Alaska. In 1880, the Chilkats granted permission to a party of prospectors to use the pass. Within three years the prospectors made a gold strike at the confluence of the Stewart and Yukon Rivers, and the trickle of whites using the Chilkoot grew into a streamlet.

Lt. Frederick Schwatka, and his expedition »sneaked« away from Vancouver, Washington, for fear that cost-cutters in Washington, D.C., would suppress the trip. The first week of June 1883, he landed at the mouth of the Dyea (Taiya River), and then, with the aid of Indians packing up to 137 pounds, crossed the Chilkoot. Schwatka proceeded down the length of the Yukon River, affixing place names as he went – to the eternal consternation of those men who came along later and wondered where the names originated. Example: Lake Lindemann, a body of water along the Chilkoot Pass trail, was named for the president of the Bremen Geographical Society in Germany. As a consequence, this appelation was to have the distinction of being misspelled by just about every stampeder who passed by it. The result is the mangled version, Lake »Linderman.«

»See if you can find another route over the pass,« suggested geologist William Ogilvie to Billy Moore, a sixtyish veteran prospector who discovered gold at Dease Creek in British Columbia and then went farther north to try his luck. Billy said okay. He selected an Indian, Tagish Charlie, as his guide and headed up the Skagway River. The year was 1887. He plotted a new route to Bennett and met Ogilvie there to tell him about it. Ogilvie didn't miss his chance to name something Schwatka missed. He called the »new« route White Pass after Thomas White, Canada's Minister of the Interior. Moore and »Tagish« Charlie returned to Skagway. Ogilvie reported Moore and Skookum Jim made the trip, thus initiating perennial confusion among the names and faces of Skookum Jim, Tagish Charlie, and Dawson Charlie. They were all from a place called Caribou Crossing (really at that time an Indian hunting and fishing camp) whose name for postal efficiency was shortened later to Carcross.

A 15-year-old Indian lad stared wide-eyed at 2 white men who walked into his village on the Klukshu River. The year was 1890, and it was the first time he had ever seen a »paleface.« The men were Jack Dalton and Edward Glave. Dalton came back alone in 1894; set up a trading post; and laid out the historic Dalton Trail over which he charged tolls during the 1898 gold rush. Glave went to Africa and was killed in a native ambush.

Thomas Martinus and George Hughes got into an argument over the layout of a baseball diamond. The dispute was a bitter one and a fight started. Martinus hauled out a knife and stabbed Hughes. Others broke up the fracas but not before Hughes was slashed. Ten stitches were needed to sew him up, and Martinus was thrown into irons. The place was Herschel Island, Yukon Territory, 180 miles north of the Arctic Circle, and the participants in the game were from American whaling ships that wintered there. It was 1894, five years after the first ship had slipped around Point Barrow looking for bowhead whales. The presence of the Americans at Herschel stirred a reaction in Ottawa, and a »show of the flag« was needed. In 1903 Northwest Mounted policemen were sent there to enforce customs regulations. Their commander was Staff Sergeant Frank Fitzgerald. Eight years later he and three companions were to die on the trail to Dawson City. Their story was to be known as »The Lost Patrol.«

The year was 1894. A Nova Scotian lost his job as a miner in Aspen, Colorado, and headed north. A year later, this man, Robert Henderson, earned the title of co-discoverer of the mammoth gold strike on Rabbit Creek, but got nothing out of it. In disgust, he returned to Aspen.

It was August 17, 1896. The rain was coming down in buckets but Jim Mason wanted some hot tea. He emerged from the refuge provided by a tarp and walked down to nearby Rabbit Creek to fill a billy can with water. In doing so he saw that the stream flowed on bedrock and consequently he studied it more closely. Something gleamed and he picked it up. It was a gold nugget. Henderson had been right. A few days before he had told Jim and his companions they might find the yellow metal in that area. Leisurely, Mason walked back to camp and told his companions of his discovery. Ignoring the rain they rushed down to take a look. They washed the gravel and got $5 to the pan. Gold was everywhere. It was *the* big strike! Jim's companions were Dawson Charlie, George Carmack, and Charlie's nephew, Patsy Henderson. The elder three staked claims, but Patsy, at 17, was too young. The name of the creek was shortly thereafter changed to Bonanza. Within 2 years, where there had been 3 humans, there were 30,000. Through it all, the confusion of names continued. Dawson Charlie was from Tagish. As a result, he was given the name Tagish Charlie by men who recorded the event. This resulted in confusing him with the other Tagish Charlie and the confusion continued through their lives and afterwards. Carmack bestowed the name Henderson on Dawson Charlie's nephew, and Charlie adopted the same name. Dawson Charlie purchased a hotel in Carcross; over-imbibed in drink one day, and fell off the bridge and drowned. The Mounties listed his passing as »death by mis-adventure.« Jim Mason kept his money and lived out a full life. Carmack left Jim's sister Kate, with whom he had been living as man and wife since 1888, and sailed to Seattle where he married a local girl and settled down to enjoy his newly found fortune. Bob Henderson was the only one not affected by the gold – he hadn't any. He borrowed a few dollars to return to Aspen where he married the sheriff's sister and returned to the Yukon with her. Not long after, the sheriff, Jack Grant, came along behind. The two men did not prosper, but they didn't starve either. Henderson died of old age. Grant's death was more spectacular. It was 1916. He worked on a gold dredge and had lunch with the crew. The beets tasted funny, but he ate them anyway, as did most of the other men. That night, at home, he complained of double vision. He became ill and in a matter of 24 hours was dead from botulism. Seventeen other men went to their graves with him in one of the worst disasters in Yukon history.

A young fellow stood, pencil in hand, in front of a hewn back wall of a cabin far up the reaches of the left fork of Henderson Creek. With some difficulty he scribbled his name, »Jack London,« then cocked his head to survey his work, and added »miner author, Jan. 27, 1898.« He grinned at the pun, and left the cabin. Thirty-eight years later trappers Iver Norback and Jack MacKenzie discovered the inscription. By this time London had been dead for 20 years, but his name had become virtually a household word throughout the world. London wrote 50 books in 18 years including »The Call of the Wild« and »Smoke Bellew« in which the same log cabin was thinly disguised as the location of lost treasure.

A woman lay under the snow. She could see the pale light of day above her, but like a person in a dream who wants to run but can't, she couldn't move. She was pinned under a blanket of ice crystals. She cried out but did not know if anyone heard. The lack of oxygen was fast draining her consciousness when a search pole jabbed her side. She winced, but it was a pain she gladly bore. She heard sounds of shovels working and finally her rescuers pulled her out more dead than alive. Her name was Anne Maxon. In a short time she was up and around. Her rescuers warned her to hurry, as there were threats of more avalanches. She hastened down the trail toward safety, but it was too late. Again she was engulfed and buried in a shroud of snow, and yet again she

was rescued. Mrs. Maxon was one of the lucky ones that April 3, 1898. More than 60 others died on Chilkoot Pass that day.

His name was Frank Nantuck. He was an Indian waiting to be hanged along with three of his brothers for killing a white man on the McClintock River in the spring of 1898. The hanging was delayed because of jurisdictional problems caused by the creating of the Yukon Territory that summer. Two of his brothers were spared the noose. They died of tuberculosis while in jail. Frank and another brother earned the dubious distinction of being among the first men hanged in the Yukon Territory.

Two men were sitting under the cover of a huge boulder. They deemed it a good refuge from a dynamite blast shortly to be set off during the building of the White Pass and Yukon Railroad. The blast went off on schedule, but the jar of the explosion caused the boulder to shift and the men were crushed beneath it. Today this stone is called Black Cross Rock. There's a postscript to the story. Shortly after the accident 2,000 railroad workers went on strike charging callousness on the part of the railroad's management for not removing the bodies of the 2 men. One of the issues was the claim that 12 men, not 2, were under the rock. Railroad officials brought forth witnesses attesting that there were, indeed, only two men under the rock. A careful assessment was made and it was found to be impractical to remove the men as the rock would have to be blown up, further disturbing their remains. The logic of this headed off more objections but the work proceeded until the railroad was completed in 1900.

The year was 1905. Clouds of mosquitoes, the perennial bane of the summer wilderness traveler in the arctic and sub-arctic regions, swarmed around a geologist while he was making a survey of the Wind River. He later wrote in his book »Son of the North«: »Here and there were small muskeg ponds and the mosquitoes were in myriads. They rose up in clouds with every step I took. I had no protection from these pests, neither head net nor mosquito dope, and from time to time as I got tired I also became almost panicky. When I felt myself beginning to run I immediately pulled up and made a small fire so that I could get some relief in the smoke. I could easily imagine a man going off his head if he should have to endure such torture for any length of time.« The man was Charles Camsell, an experienced woodsman and bush traveler, and the first geologist to make the journey from Dawson City to Fort McPherson by way of the Stewart, Wind and Peel Rivers.

It was 1906. H. W. McWhorter's vision went beyond that of chasing the eternal rainbow with only a pot of gold at the end of it. He kept an experienced eye out for other minerals, and one day spotted a silver-lead outcrop 3 miles up Galena Creek about 40 miles north of the present town of Mayo. He staked it, little realizing he was treading on ground that would eventually turn up one of the richest silver mines in the world.

Trader John K. Tom, a Tlingit Indian dressed in a Stetson, suit jacket and vest, white shirt and tie, pants created like knife blades, shoes gleaming, and sporting a gold watch and chain to match, journeyed to Juneau, Alaska from his home at Tagish, Yukon in 1908. He was living proof that a native could make it in a »white man's« world. He made a fortune as a trader of furs. He was not the only one of his race to demonstrate capabilities as a businessman. Later, such men as Joe Netro, of Old Crow, and George Johnston, of Teslin, did equally well.

Fred Whitehead was crossing a glacier in 1910 when he crashed through a snow bridge into a crevasse. The fall knocked him out. He finally gained consciousness and noted from the fuzzy light filtering through the hole he made through the snow crust, that he was perched on a chunk of ice jammed between two sides of the crevasse. He was the meat in an icy sandwich. Either way, right or left, was nothing but yawning blackness. Stunned, he shook his head in disbelief. This happened to other people but not to him. He reached behind him, plucked a prospector's pick from a loop in his overalls, and began chopping his way up the ice cliff. It was 30 feet and he climbed at the rate of 5 feet an hour. He neared the top and the pick slipped from his grasp. He snared it out of the air with the acumen of a baseball player, and then sweated and trembled for half an hour. He started again and made it to safety. Seventy years later a tourist saw a man cashing in gold at the Bank of Commerce in Dawson City. She asked a resident who he was. The resident told her – Fred Whitehead.

A strange procession struggled up Haystack Mountain south of Dawson City in 1915. One group carried an oblong box, and another struggled with a barrel. A passerby wondered if they had all gone mad. No, they were merely carrying out the last wish of Sam Haffstad, who prospected the area surrounding Haystack and who always wanted to climb it but never found the time. He left $1,000 in his will to provide for a celebration if he was buried on top of the mountain. They did the job and drank up the thousand.

Fritz Guder, a young immigrant from Germany, half-starved, plodded through the wilderness of the legendary Nahanni country. His pack dogs cornered a bull moose. Without a rifle, Fritz bound a knife to a pole and stabbed the moose again and again. The battle continued for six hours as his dogs kept the moose at bay. Finally, Guder finished off the bleeding moose with an axe. Twenty-three years later World War II came along and Guder's rifle was taken from him because he was an enemy alien. Undaunted, Fritz carved himself a bow and arrows and continued hunting. Today he can be found working his gold claim 30 miles west of Carmacks.

A middle-aged ambulance driver lay huddled in a ditch by the side of a road in France, his vehicle riddled by shrapnel. It was World War I. The year was 1916 and, as he witnessed the blood and gore and the folly of that attack and of that war, he kept his sanity by writing poetry. The result of this was one of his great books, »Rhymes of a Red Cross Man.« Elsewhere, half way around the world, he was known for other poems such as: »The Spell of the Yukon,« »The Shooting of Dan McGrew,« and »The Cremation of Sam McGee.« The man was Robert Service, who achieved immortality through his poems about the Yukon. He lived to the ripe old age of 84.

A young Indian lad by the name of Johnny Johns in Carcross, Yukon aspired to be a big game guide. He wrote and re-wrote an ad and sent it in to »Outdoor Life« magazine. It cost him six dollars to run it for three months in 1917. A hunter wrote to Johnny and he signed him up for the fall season. That was the beginning. Johns went on to become one of the most celebrated guides in the world, and before he retired, his clients included royalty, company presidents, and celebrities from all walks of life.

It was a gala day for most of the people aboard the *Princess Sophia.* She sailed from Skagway, Alaska the night of October 24, 1918. Most of the 349 people on board, with the exception of the 61 crewmen, were from Dawson City. It was a time of the year to be happy. The mining season was over and the passengers, many of whom were miners and their families, looked forward to a winter's relaxation in warmer climes. In addition, the bloodiest war in history was almost at a close, giving that much more reason for celebrating. Signals Private A.W. McQueen had his share of fun that first night out and was preparing for bed at 3.00 A.M. when the ship slammed into Vanderbilt Reef, 65 miles south of Skagway. There was some panic, and two ladies fainted, but the excitement subsided as the boat came to rest on an even keel atop the reef. The captain then made his fatal decision – to wait until another ship of the same line arrived to take the passengers off. He turned down four smaller boats offering help. Wrote McQueen on his second night aboard the stricken ship: »The decks are icy, and this wreck has all the marks of a movie stage setting. All we lack is the hero – I'm going to quit and see if I can rustle a bucket and a line to get some sea water and wash in it. We are mighty lucky we are not all buried in sea water.« Unfortunately for McQueen, in a short time he was one of the 349 persons who went down with the vessel in one of the worst sea disasters in history. The only survivor was a dog. A giant storm which arose during the night swept the ship off the reef to a watery grave. Along with it went one quarter of the population of Dawson City.

A Dall sheep rambled over the lip of the hill and Louis Beauvette cursed his hunting luck that day in 1919. To lose the ram when he was so close was maddening. Beauvette sat down to rest and immediately spotted an outcrop of galena shining in the sun. He and three friends staked the Roulette, Keno, Scotty, Pinochle, Wolverine, and Rico claims. A stampede followed; 1,000 claims were staked and $300,000 worth of silver and lead were taken out in one year. This was the beginning of the United Keno Hill Mine, one of the richest in the world and a mine that is still in production.

White man's technology held no fears for George Johnston of Teslin. He bought a Chevrolet car in 1928 and had it shipped to him. Needing a road on which to run the car, he built his own three miles in the middle of the Yukon wilderness. He charged people a dollar a ride, then painted the car white and took a record harvest of wolves running the car over the frozen Teslin Lake that winter. Fourteen years later, American army engineers building the Alaska Highway (Alcan Highway) reached Teslin, and, to their amazement found three miles of road already done for them.

In 1932, Barney West got his last wish. The jailer gave him a bottle of whisky. He held it up saying: »*Johnny Walker* put me in here and *Johnny Walker* is taking me out of here.« He took a big gulp and then walked to the scaffold. The trap was sprung, and the High Point, North Carolina man became the last person hanged in the Yukon Territory. His crime was the drunken bludgeoning of an old man whom he thought had a fortune in gold hidden in his cabin.

Trapper »Albert Johnson« was gunned down on the ice of the Eagle River in one of the most bizarre shoot-outs and chases in the history of the Royal Canadian Mounted Police. His crime was the shooting of a Mountie, and the year was also 1932. To this day no one knows who the trapper was or »from whence he came.«

In the twenties and thirties, children of river residents set out for school in Dawson City by floating downriver on rafts. They killed moose along the way to help supply the school with meat.

What happened to Anton Leland? It was the spring of 1934 and Arthur Zimmerlie, who ran a trading post at Russell Creek, a small community far up the Macmillan River, was on his annual trip to Fort Selkirk on the Yukon River. He reached Leland's cabin, and, as is customary in the north, hailed him from some distance, but received no answer. Zimmerlie approached closer and yelled again. Still no answer. He opened the cabin door and found a pot of warm coffee on the stove. The fire was still smoldering, and a plate of eggs was still warm. Puzzled, he looked around. Leland's gear had not been removed. The only thing missing was his rifle. The visitor walked out and saw the trapper's water bucket down by the river. Falling snow had covered all tracks. Zimmerlie noted a hole in the ice where Leland drew water, but it was too small for him to have slipped through it. At first the trader supposed Leland spotted a caribou and ran across the river to shoot it and fell through the ice, but there was no evidence of a break. To Zimmerlie, Leland's disappearance was almost too perfect to be an accident. What, then, did happen to him? Suicide? Murder? To this day no one knows.

A plane crashed in the wilderness in 1936 and its pilot surveyed the damage. The propeller was broken. He proceeded to hew another one out of a log, attached it to the plane, and flew out. The propeller was shipped to the Canadian air museum. The pilot was George Dalziel. Forty-six years later he is still flying planes.

A youth of 18 worked in the slop and mud of a gold dredge operation at Dominion Creek in 1938. The shovel work was back-breaking but not enough to suppress his dream of putting the history of the Klondike stampede on paper some day. He did that and more. His »Klondike Fever« became a best seller, and he wrote 28 more books before he was 60. His name is Pierre Berton.

Robert Martin pined for his girlfriend in 1939. He lived in Mayo and she was 400 miles north of him at Aklavik in the Northwest Territories. Every last inch was uncharted wilderness. Little can stop a love-struck lad, and Robert was no exception. He set out with his dog team and was soon swallowed up in the wilderness. Nothing was heard from him and he was thought to be lost forever. Forty days later he emerged from the forest at his destination. There was a happy ending. He visited his girlfriend and eventually married her.

War clouds gathered and the storm burst. World War II began. The American army was ordered north to build a highway from British Columbia to Alaska. They slashed it through in nine months of 1942. The next year another contingent initiated the Canol oil pipeline, and a year later oil was flowing from Norman Wells, Northwest Territories to Whitehorse. It operated less than a year and was abandoned when the war ended in 1945.

Whitehorse was selected as capital of the Yukon in 1951. The move was completed in 1953, the same year a dam was constructed blocking the Yukon River above Whitehorse. It provided power for the new capital.

Snowshoe-clad Joe Henry, a Loucheux Indian, led a worm-like procession of Caterpillar tractors to open up the Peel Plateau to oil drillers in 1952. It was the end of the trapping season and the cagy Indian led the tractors to his traps which he picked up and deposited on the sleds pulled by the mechanical monsters. Eight years later he was at it again, leading surveyors who were plotting the first section of the Dempster Highway. They got lost and the disgusted guide had to find them.

The Alaska Highway gave access to those who otherwise could not afford to go north. Al Kulan, a prospector, journeyed up the road with his wife and family. He was broke, but was grubstaked in 1953 by Burt and Ellen Law, who owned a roadhouse near Squanga Lake. The Laws and Kulans were both about broke when Al took one last prospecting trip. He and Arthur John of Ross River were camped near Little Salmon when he found an old prospector's pick. He figured it was a sign of good luck. It was. A month later he discovered a lead-zinc ore body; staked it; and made $150,000 for himself and his partners. Al blew the money on a laundromat and went back again to search for more metals. Ten years later lightning struck a second time, again in the presence of another native, Joe Ladue. He found another lead-zinc zone even larger than the first discovery. It was to become the half billion dollar Cyprus-Anvil complex, and to make him a multi-millionaire.

Events came in a hurry in the sixties. During 1967 and 1968: the first jet airplane service was inaugurated at the Whitehorse airport; New Imperial Mines (copper), and Clinton Creek asbestos mines went into production. They were followed by Cyprus-Anvil at Faro.

In 1979 the Dempster Highway was completed. It was the first all-weather public road to cross the Arctic Circle in North America and the first to reach the arctic sea.

Shortly after that the Skagway Road opened giving quick access to the sea for dwellers of the southern Yukon.

In 1980 it all came together for Dean Elston, construction boss for the giant Alaska Highway gas pipeline project. He completed the survey for the 56 inch pipe which will eventually carry the gas. Among other Yukon jobs he served in a supervisory capacity with the Canol line, the Alaska Highway, and the first section of the Dempster in 1960. He had grown up with the country and said: »Let the future care for itself.«

Today, many young adventurers seek to relive the challenge faced by turn-of-the-century gold seekers who had to climb the Chilkoot Pass from Skagway's neighbor, Dyea, to Bennett Lake.

Skagway, Alaska, populated now by 770 people, once hosted some 20,000 fortune seekers from around the world, as they prepared for their long, dangerous journey to the northern Klondike gold fields.

A White Pass & Yukon train leaves the Canadian border to head south to Skagway.

Patterned gold dredge tailings from played-out gold mines pile up beside the Klondike River near Dawson City, with the Klondike High-way cutting through.

David Rhode of Dawson City with fireweed, the Yukon's flower emblem.

Gold panning has become lucrative again with the rising gold prices; and any visitor to the Yukon or to Alaska has ample opportunity to try his luck.

A lone coyote travels snow-covered river valleys and forests in search of food.

The wolf, often described in the stories of Jack London, is part of the Yukon's natural heritage as well.

The Ogilvie
Mountains, nature's
winter paradise.

▷

Hawk owl, night watcher of the northern forests.

Snowshoe hare.

Dall sheep rut: four rams engage in a shoving match.

Two hikers in the serenity of early morning wander across an alpine meadow of the »frontal« ranges of the St. Elias Mountains.

Yellow arctic poppies at the shores of the Beaufort Sea.

Heavy weather in the Ogilvie Mountains along the Dempster Highway, named after Corporal Dempster of the Royal North West Mounted Police, who

led a party north from Dawson City by dog sled in the winter of 1911 in search of the ill-fated Fitzgerald patrol.

Red fox family
playing.

Steel traps on an
Indian trapper's
cabin.

Quiet waters and forests alongside the Klondike Highway.

Fall colors along the South Canol Road, which runs through country of startling beauty and abundant wildlife, where names such as Quiet

Lake and Caribou Mountain attest to the peaceful solitude of this wilderness setting.

First September snow on the mountains, through which the »Top of the World Highway« between Dawson City and Alaska has been built for summer travel.

A flock of trumpeter swans migrating to southern quarters over Marsh Lake, which, like Tagish Lake and Lake Bennett, is part of the Yukon River's headwaters.

Fishing for trout on Fox Lake at the Klondike Highway.

The Palace Grand
Theatre and its
»Gaslight Follies« in
Dawson City, the
heart of the Klondike
gold rush. Klondike –
even the name spells
adventure: gold
nuggets; honky-tonk
piano players and
high kicking can-can
girls; and blackjack
and roulette at
Diamond Tooth
Gertie's, the only
(legal) gambling hall
of its type in Canada.

The Dempster
Highway in the
loneliness of the
Richardson Mountains
close to the border of
the Northwest
Territories.

Whitewater kayaking
on the Tutshi River,
flowing from B.C.
into the Yukon
watershed.

Wherever there is a
stream, there are fish
in abundance to be
caught, as here in the
Frances River
alongside the Robert
Campbell Highway,

named after one of
Canada's fur trade
explorers of the
Hudson's Bay
Company.

THE YUKON TODAY by Andrew Hume

Ever since this wedge-shaped slice of northern wilderness known as the Yukon first appeared on Canadian maps as a distinct and individual territory back in 1898, it has been plagued with an identity crisis. And although more is known today about this land and the people who make it their home than was perhaps ever known before, many of the myths, the false romanticisms and the misconceptions still dangle like some unwanted thread from the true cultural, geographic and environmental fabric which makes up the north.

The Yukon, as it is geographically recognized today, was born in a frenzied time. Sparked by the discovery of gold in the waning years of the 19th century, tens of thousands of men and women began flooding into the unknown north like souls possessed. The mad search for the precious yellow metal which lay hidden in the stream beds and valleys of the Klondike brought mostly foreigners into a far-off land they knew nothing of. As a protective measure designed to ensure the area would not be ravaged and exploited by this onslaught of foreign gold seekers, the Canadian government hastily drew out the boundaries for this new territory of the dominion. The southern boundary of the territory sweeps for almost 600 miles along the 60th parallel, while the northern border, washed by the Artic Ocean above the 69th parallel, narrows to a bottleneck little more than 100 miles wide between the Yukon's western neighbor, Alaska, and the sprawling Northwest Territories to the east.

The Yukon is mostly an unpeopled land, a land where unspoiled wilderness has lease over almost 190,000 square miles of the Canadian north. Its total population today is about 24,500, including 6,000 Indians, but the majority of people live in or near Whitehorse, the Yukon's capital.

In the northernmost reaches of the territory ancient mountains, eroded over countless millennia by the constant caress of nature, rise from the surface of the placid tundra into softly rounded humps adding a sensuous element to a sweeping vista of land and sky. These are the Richardson Mountains. Spilling out of the high north like a gently rolling sea, they straddle that imaginary line which forms the boundary with the Northwest Territories. These mountains are the hoary spawning ground for a myriad of streams which tumble out of the highlands and feed the major waterways like the Peel, the Porcupine and the Mackenzie.

High to the northwest run the British Mountains which form a rocky barrier across the top of the territory and slope gently northward into the sweeping flatlands which make up the Yukon's only coastline. Interrupting this constant flow of the land, rivers etch their course like twisted tangles of blue-green ribbons. The largest of these rivers, such as the Firth and the Malcolm, spread out into huge fans as they empty into the Beaufort Sea.

The fragility of the environment in this region is ever apparent, especially where the marks of man scar this otherwise untouched wilderness domain. And in the brief arctic summer every living thing seems to squeeze the juices of life from the land. A kaleidoscopic array of wild-flowers bursts forth in a fury of life with the coming of the perpetual summer daylight, completely changing the tone and visible texture of the landscape in a matter of days. This arctic coastal region is also the summer calving ground for the barrenground caribou which trickle north in small herds from their winter feeding grounds 400 miles to the south, eventually flowing together into one massive river of wildlife. This is the Porcupine caribou herd. Estimated to number 120,000 animals, it is one of the last remaining wildlife spectacles of its kind to be found anywhere on the North American continent. Reminiscent of the great herds of bison which once roamed freely across this country, the caribou now face similar danger from the encroachment of man.

Other wildlife species also coexist within this harsh northern environment. The powerful grizzly and polar bear, wolverine and wolf, arctic fox and a huge variety of migratory birds crowd the land with new life which has been seemingly missing throughout the dark and often tortuous winter. It can be an unforgiving land, where the slightest mistake can mean the difference between life and death for both man and beast.

A hundred miles to the south, near the tiny Loucheux Indian settlement of Old Crow on the Porcupine River, is found one of the most unusual environmental features in the Yukon – the Old Crow Flats. This huge marshy flatland is pockmarked with thousands of small lakes and a confused knot of meandering waterways.

And like the huge flocks of waterfowl which come to nest here each summer, so do the people of Old Crow make an annual migration to this watershed to hunt for the rich and supple fur of the muskrat.

In the central region of the territory, the Ogilvie Mountains erupt with an apparent violence from valley floors, their jagged peaks scraping the sky.

The mood of the Yukon landscape changes dramatically with the seasons, for when the tempestuous arctic storm fronts of winter move with their ruthless brutality across the far north, the scene can be transformed into a blinding, white void. Thirty and forty-mile an hour blizzards can churn up the elements creating one of the most inhospitable environments on earth where exposed human flesh can freeze in a matter of minutes. It is a land which commands respect.

Coursing diagonally across the southwestern Yukon and on through Alaska to the Bering Sea, the Yukon River winds from its headwaters in the southern Yukon and northern British Columbia for 2,000 miles across the vast wilderness. Constituting the fifth largest river basin in North America, the Yukon River drains the network of large southern lakes which straddle the B.C./Yukon border. A myriad of major tributaries and small streams feeds this primary watercourse, swelling it to five times its originating size before it crosses into neighboring Alaska. During spring break-up the Yukon River is an awesome sight. With a sudden heave the river breaks the bonds of winter and in a matter of hours can turn from a flat, frozen highway into a churning mass of snow and ice. Enormous chunks of blue-green ice grate against one another, setting off an ominous rumbling thunder in an astounding show of brute force. Like an awakening giant, the river is jolted back to life with one great sigh.

In some regions of the territory the new life of spring never arrives. Atop the lofty pinnacles of Canada's highest peaks, the changing of the seasons is of little significance. These mammoth protrusions of snow, ice and rock are the St. Elias Mountains which remain clad in their wintry cloaks as the lower valleys awaken from their winter slumber with a sudden brilliance of color and new life.

Wedged into the extreme southwestern corner of the Yukon, the St. Elias Mountains march in distant ranks. At the heart is Mt. Logan, the roof of Canada at 19,850 feet, rising with unquestionable majesty from the perpetual snowfields which surround its base and spread out like a great frozen desert. The largest non-polar icefield in the world sets the stage for this impressive mountain barrier. The massive bulks of glaciers spill through the mountain passes on their relentless, grinding course toward the valley bottoms. With the slow melt of summer, the largest of these surging, icy mammoths calve huge turquoise icebergs into the silty, shallow lakes which form the headwaters for the numerous rivers which rush with determined destiny from their frigid birthplaces.

The diverse geographical composition of the Yukon's natural elements creates a land of stark contrast and striking panoramas. Often blessed with scenes of breathless beauty, this land of wild rivers, rugged mountains and rolling plains is a land to be cherished, respected and preserved.

Man has been occupying the far reaches of the northern Yukon perhaps longer than anywhere else on the North American continent. Recent archeological finds near Old Crow date man's presence in the region to almost 30,000 years ago when nomadic tribesmen roamed freely across the landscape.

The recent settlement of the territory over the past 100 year has been but a mere twinkle in the history of man. Yet the encroachment of civilization over the last century has irrevocably altered the lifestyles and value systems of the Yukon's original inhabitants. From a historical perspective it has been a sudden and radical transformation. The old ways, established and refined over thousands of years, had passed forever with the dawning of the new age of civilization.

It began with a slow trickle as the white explorers, fur traders and prospectors began making historically significant inroads into the Yukon's uncharted wilderness. But with the discovery of the region's mineral wealth the floodgates of humanity were opened and the newcomers poured north by the tens of thousands. In half a century the metamorphosis was complete, the Yukon would never again be the unknown, untrodden land it had been since time immemorial. The last frontier had been settled with the coming of modern man.

Today, Yukon's native peoples are still fighting for a place in this contemporary society which has overtaken them. Some have chosen to accept the new ways while others scorn those whom they label as exploiters of the Yukon's land and natural wealth. Despite some bitter resentment which still exists between the cultures of new and old, there is also a new consciousness, a realization that the system is here to stay and an understanding that a peaceful co-existence requires mutual knowledge, communication and a willingness to accept and respect varying lifestyles and values.

Brought up by this new system, but keeping a sharp focus on their historical roots, today's young Indian leaders are articulate, aware and capable of dealing with rapidly changing issues and concerns in this new, shared society. To a limited degree, they have won positions of influence in the arenas of politics and business and command a strong voice for their people.

But there are also those who have been ruined by these new social structures. Caught between cultures, their social mores have become clouded and confused, their feeling of belonging has fallen somewhere between the cracks of time. Choked and blinded by the dust as the world sped off before them on an unknown course, drunkenness, poverty, despair and self-doubt are all that is left for some. Yet their case is not unique, for every society has those who are left to flounder in the wake of rapid progress, losing their sense of place and purpose, unable to keep up with social change.

For the majority, progress and development does

and will continue, bringing with it a prosperous lifestyle for those who have learned to temper prosperity with reason and self-control.

Mining, the industry which launched the Yukon into the 20th century and the consciousness of the nation, remains the territory's economic mainstay. At the turn of the century it was the promise of gold which lured people north. Today it is lead-zinc, copper, silver and the untold potential wealth of oil and natural gas as well as the seduction of escaping southern metropolitan life for a closer co-existence with nature.

The development and growth of mines, towns and transportation corridors continues to creep ever wider into previously untouched regions leaving undeniable evidence of a human presence. But with these great technological advancements, attitudes too have experienced a radical change since men with picks and shovels first began turning the north's untrodden soil in search of mineral wealth. A renewed appreciation and understanding of the environment and the fragile ecosystem which exist in the north has fostered stricter legislation and a closer watch over those industries which develop and extract the natural resources of the land.

It is this appreciation of the natural world which keeps many Yukoners where they are, despite their chronic complaints about the disturbingly high cost of living, the distorted southern impression of the north and the seemingly uncaring political attitudes of the federal government. The ability to escape the workaday world and the nuances of society's social and political games is a freedom many find worth paying for.

It's the search for that freedom and the lust for something unique which draws hundreds of thousands of people north each summer. They are not developers, fortune seekers or escapists from southern society, but tourists, who constitute the second largest injection into the Yukon's economy and form the lifeblood for many northern businesses.

Today, it's an annual human migration of as many as 400,000 people. The mountain passes have been notched by highways, the elements tempered by the man-made cocoons of automobiles and airplanes and the silence of the wilderness broken by the throb of engines.

It may be only the thin wisp of a jet stream etching a line across an azure sky, but the presence of man cannot be denied. Still, the beaten tracks are few and the open reaches of the land immense. There are still places where lifetimes pass that no man sees, where events of nature unfold and leave no legacy to be spoken through human lips, where the destiny of the natural world is determined solely by time and the elements.

The Yukon possesses a diverse cross-section of cultures and value systems which give it a unique social fiber in this modern age. It's a land where a hunter or trapper can still make his living by following the age-old traditions established by his forefathers, but it's also a land where a business executive can find a comfortable place in society. While people share the physical amenities of urban life and the peaceful solitude of nature, each can return to his chosen lifestyle without fear of social reproach.

Politically, the Yukon is emerging as an integral member in the Canadian family and the quest for individual recognition and an equal place at the table is becoming a dominant force which shapes the future of the territory and determines its place within Canada. As the Yukon's population continues to swell and the prospects of major industrial developments gain momentum, Yukoners are beginning to demand more self-control over their economic, political and cultural destiny. The political maturation of the Yukon has meant a stronger voice for northerners within the halls of Parliament and helped to loosen the yoke of colonialism which has determined the direction and evolution of the territory ever since its borders were first carved out of the Canadian northwest.

For northerners, the struggle for equal recognition is by no means over, but the winds of change are helping to clear away many of the clouded impressions of this vast and dynamic region of Canada.

Yet in the end, it is still the last frontier. Its destiny now, depends on the manipulation of man.

INDIAN VERSES FROM THE YUKON

WHO OWNS THE YUKON?

Who owns the Yukon?
Who owns this land?
The White? The Indian?
Who has it in his hands?
I say, »Neither!«
For »god« created Earth.
He owns the World
Right from its birth.
Why fight over something
We do not own?
Anyway, who has the right
To take something from our Creator?
But »they« will pay later.
I feel sorry for those
Who don't understand this.
»god« is the Great Spirit.
And everything is »HIS.«

by Emily Shorty

A CALL FOR JUSTICE

White man, only time is between us.
Once in the time long gone you lived in caves,
You used stone axes, you clothed yourself in skin,
You too feared the dark, fled the unknown.
Go back! remember your own Alcheringa
When lightning was still magic and you hid
From terrible thunder rolling in the sky.
White superior race, only time is between us –
As some are grown up and others yet children,
Waiting for time to help us
As time helped you.

Author unknown

NATIVE CHILD

Oh! native child of this timeless land
Build your dreams and your castles in the sand.
Though your future may seem empty and bare,
Burden not the mind with worry and care.

Ponder not the reasons and the why's
Just look for beauty through innocent eyes.
Don't think of the misery that daily haunts,
Or the other society's vicious taunts.

Live all the joys that only innocents can.
When you have a colored skin, black, brown or tan,
Too soon you'll grow to youth
And know all the heartbreak in the naked truth.

Walk the pathways free from sin
An innocent child with colored skin.
For too soon hatred you'll understand,
Native child of this timeless land.

Author unknown

ENJOY YOURSELF!

Our Yukon of many faces,
Many names, and many places,
Take our hands to new beginnings,
Planet clean and bright as day.

Endless miles of untouched beauty,
Enchanting thoughts, the lover's duty,
Endless rows of soaring mountains,
Uncut timber, clearbrook fountains.

Here is life or here is dying,
The only sin is lack of trying.
Grab your picks, and grab your shovels,
Dig your burrows, build your hovels.

Each year's better, each year's stronger,
Next year's burrows will be longer.
Swirling streams of pure white snow,
Cleanse our children, help them grow.

Learn to live life, learn to take it,
You can't buy it, you can't fake it.
How can you know, until you've tried,
Try again, and keep on trying …

A. Nieman

Whitehorse, the bustling capital city since 1953, serves as a center for transportation, communication and supplies for the Yukon Territory and other areas of northern Canada. The SS *Klondike,* pulled up to the banks of the Yukon River, is one of the last remaining sternwheelers and recalls the era when riverboats were the only means of long-distance transportation for passengers and supplies in this northern frontier.

Single-engine floatplane dropping supplies for hikers in the Donjek River area.

Supply helicopter at a mining camp in front of the craggy peaks of the Ogilvie Mountains.

The Alaska Highway, 1,520 miles in length from Dawson Creek, B.C., to Fairbanks, Alaska, was punched through virgin Yukon and Alaska wilderness as a strategic military supply road during a 9-month-period in 1942, when Japanese forces threatened an invasion of Alaska.

The »Alcan« is both a vital transportation artery and a scenic adventure route.

A main attraction at Watson Lake, first Yukon stop on the Alaska Highway, are the »Sign Posts,« a weather worn collection of hometown and auto signs, begun by a homesick soldier during the highway's construction.

The Alaska Highway between Whitehorse and Haines Junction with the St. Elias Mountains ahead.

Mary Lindahl jogging
at −35°F to keep fit.

Hoar frost in the
Yukon.

Giant Kaskawulsh
Glacier, part of the
largest nonpolar
icefield in the world,
in the St. Elias
Mountains of Kluane
National Park, with
powerful Mt. Logan,
at 19,850 ft. Canada's
highest peak.

▷

The fall colors of the
Richardson Mountains
in the north of the
Yukon; a very large
number of barren
ground caribou live
here and on the
plains to the west
and north.

»This is the law of the Yukon, that only the Strong shall thrive;
That surely the Weak shall perish, and only the Fit survive.
Dissolute, damned and despairful, crippled and palsied and slain.
This is the will of the Yukon, –
Lo, how she makes it plain!«

Robert Service
THE LAW OF THE YUKON

Robert Service; a bankteller and poet who staked his claim in the Yukon not for gold but for the riches it held in beauty and inspiration. With his words Service described the Yukon he knew at the turn of the century when men bet their lives for that paydirt: gold.
Although times have changed, the Law of the Yukon remains the same. Away from the city streets there lies a vast and beckoning land. Modern technology has made it easier in many ways but it still takes a unique breed to challenge the Yukon.
The tales that follow are all true. Some have been related to me by the people who actually experienced them.

AN EXTRACTION'S AS GOOD AS AN AIR RESCUE

»Well, if you want to know what my name is it's G.I. Cameron, better known as Cam. Well, I came down south here into Whitehorse in 1949. Before that I was, of course, up in the north end of the territory. I was downriver at Fort Selkirk for 14 years with the Mounted Police at the time, the Royal Canadian Mounted Police, of course.«
There were no doctors or dentists in the outposts back then. Cam remembers life being quite simple when he was stationed in Selkirk.
»I generally kept a pair of pliers in my pocket and if somebody wanted their teeth pulled, why you'd pull them. We didn't have to freeze them or anything like that. In the winter if they opened their mouth too wide they'd freeze them anyways.« A smile creeps across Cam's face and he lets go a chuckle.
Before Fort Selkirk, in the mid-twenties, Cam was stationed in Dawson City. Another officer at the station was a man by the name of Andy Cruikshanks. He had once been an air force pilot but he joined the police and went to Dawson City when World War I was over.
But Cruiky always had a yen to fly again. He and Cam toyed with the idea of having a plane service in the north and pondered how to raise the money.

Soon afterwards Cam was transfered east of Dawson to the Keno detachment. Before he knew it, Cruiky had managed to raise some money and was in California having the *Queen of the Yukon* built.
In the same factory, next to *Queen of the Yukon*, was Charles A. Lingbergh's plane, *Spirit of St. Louis*.
Both planes were completed about the same time. Lindbergh went east to make the first nonstop solo flight across the Atlantic and Cruikshanks came back to the Yukon.
When Cruiky was flying in the territory he was the best pilot the Yukon had. He was also the only private pilot and he was the first.
Cam was still in Keno when he received a message from the Mayo detachment that Cruiky was down on a flight from Whitehorse. It was the first snowstorm of the year and Cruikshanks had one passenger with him. He hadn't reported in. Cam was to go to Mayo to begin a search by dog team.
Loading up the car with his three dogs and a toboggan, he headed into Mayo that night. When he arrived he was wishing he had a fourth dog because he'd have to break trail all the way. The officer on duty at Mayo jumped into action. He opened the door, stepped out on the street and grabbed the first dog he saw. It wasn't exactly what Cam had in mind but at least it was a dog and so, »Freckles« joined the team. Early the next morning Cam set out on the long trail heading for Whitehorse. About noon he stopped for lunch at a stagecoach shelter. As he put on the soup he spotted two bedraggled men coming down the trail. They were Cruiky and his passenger.
On their feet they wore bags and on their heads they sported a couple of pairs of ladies' silk stockings. It was about −25°F and they'd been traveling most of the night after being forced down in the storm.
The incident became the Yukon's first air rescue.

WOMAN ALONE

Winter was on in the Yukon. It was the end of October, 1979. Susan Yeates was working alone as winter watchman at a mining camp about 65 miles into the bush from Dawson City. The only access to the camp was by helicopter.
It should have been past the time for worrying about bears but when Sue woke one morning she found evidence that a hungry bear had been at her doorstep during the night.
Sue prepared for a return visit from the bear and that evening, at about 9.30, she heard him banging on the stovepipe outside.
She picked up the only gun the camp had left her. It was a 30-30 rifle, great for shooting smaller game but not much good when dealing with a starving grizzly bear.

Carefully Sue opened her door and peered out. The night was black and it seemed the harder she looked the blacker it got. This was a strange phenomenon because when Sue looked up she saw the sky was clear and bright with stars. As her eyes came down to search for the bear once more she was stunned by the sight of his massive head silhouetted against the sky.

Instantly she realized she was too close to him to raise her rifle without nudging him in the stomach so she took a step back and fired a shot. As she rushed to load another shell into the chamber the bear lowered himself from the housewall onto all fours. But Sue couldn't fire again. Horror overcame her as she discovered her gun was jammed.

Slamming the door in the bear's face she struggled desperately to unjam the gun. Beads of sweat rose beneath her mop of red hair. Outside she could hear the grizzly thrashing against the cabin. Only a thin door separated her from that hungry – and now wounded – giant.

By strong will or good fortune, miraculously the gun unjammed and once again Sue swung the door open, ready for the match. She knew it would be the last competition. One of them would have to come out the victor. Outside the cabin she came face to face with the grizzly.

He was just six feet away and down in charge position. Without hesitating, Sue let go a shot. The bear dropped.

It was actually Sue's first shot that had killed the grizzly. Entering through his chin the bullet had lodged in his brain. But bears have a nervous system that can stay active 11 to 15 minutes after a fatal wound; just like a chicken with its head cut off.

The second shot had entered the bear's ear, traveled down the spinal chord and lodged in the backbone between his shoulder blades. That shot took out his nervous system and without a sigh or a moan the grizzly fell to the ground.

Measuring him later, Sue discovered that when up on his hind legs he stood almost ten feet tall, twice her height. His weight was estimated at 700 pounds and he was 21 years old, one of the oldest bears on record in the territory.

But that bear had kept an ace in the hole for Sue. After a couple of dinners of bear steak she contracted trichinosis.

A few days later she lay delirious in her cabin, the bear's parasites ravaging her nervous system. Perhaps he had won after all.

With her last strength Sue wired up the spare parts of a shortwave radio to the battery of an old truck and desperately put out a plea for help. In the early hours of the morning a fishing boat in the Bering Sea picked up the message. The next day a rescue helicopter found her unconscious in the cabin.

Sue spent a six-month recovery period in the East before she felt she'd finally won the fight with that bear.

LED BY FOREBODING

It was black and blustery that night when Number 2 Engine was southward bound, pulling a full load of passengers. Outside the train a wicked storm beat on the valley. The engineer was concerned. Beside him sat his little daughter.

As the windswept rain pounded the train he peered into the darkness. He thought about being home that night, out of the dreadful storm.

The trip from Whitehorse, Yukon, to Skagway, Alaska, was nothing new for him. He'd traveled it many times on the White Pass and Yukon Route rail line. But that night something kept nagging at him. He worried about high water but could see nothing so he kept the train going, slicing through the night and bearing down on Second Crossing, one of the bridges that crosses the river.

Suddenly he had a premonition. Dynamiting the air brakes, he screeched the train to a halt adding chaos to the storm that already raged. As the conductor came up to the engine demanding to know why the train had been stopped, the engineer and his fireman stepped into the night and walked ahead.

What they saw sent cold shivers into their boots. The bridge was gone. Had the train continued on, it would have gone careening over the edge into the swollen and frothing river below. An untold number of lives would have been lost.

The engineer never knew what made him stop the train that night.

TO LIVE, HE MUST CRAWL

For over 50 years Moe Grant has lived in the Yukon. Several times he has challenged the territory and everytime he's won.

It was back in 1950, as a young man of 20, that Moe defied the Yukon for the first time. He had barely begun his lifetime career as a bush pilot and he had just bought his first plane in '49. In those days aircraft were relatively ill-equipped. One fuel line and one fuel tank were all his little Tiger Moth could boast.

On February 22 Moe began a flight home to Whitehorse from Atlin, British Columbia, a tiny village just south of the Yukon border. He was only 15 or 20 miles out of Atlin when he discovered the fuel line on his plane had broken. Below him the mountains stretched unendingly. There was nowhere to go and he was losing altitude. With the fuel supply cut off to his engine the mountain was master. It beckoned him closer and closer.

But Moe refused to succumb. Keeping the nose lifted he ground the bottom of the plane into the snow. Hidden rocks tore out the undercarriage but the landing had been a success. Moe was alive – although his left foot was broken and his right ankle dislocated.

He was at the 5,000 foot level and it was cold. On the barren mountainside Moe had little protection that night. The metal of the plane ached in the cold as did his body. Tearing some fabric off the bottom of the wings Moe managed to start a small fire but it wasn't long before his left foot froze and that natural anaesthetic eased the pain of the break.

As the sun rose the next morning Moe knew he had to find better protection. The day before several aircraft had flown overhead but the frantic waving of his engine tent couldn't attract their attention. The huge expanse of land made Moe and his plane nothing more than another rock in the wilderness. What lay ahead for him was a 1,000 foot descent to the timberline. The trees would provide protection from the wind and he could keep a fire going with the matches he had in his pocket.

With his two helpless feet Moe began to slither, slide and crawl down the mountain in snow that was waist deep. As the day warmed the glistening white became slushy. By the time Moe finally reached his destination the matches in his pocket were uselessly wet. He would have to spend the night without fire. Curling up beneath a tree Moe prepared to wait. Most of the coming days he spent just lying there watching the skies or sleeping. On occasion he would rise to stretch and gather some snow to quench his nagging thirst.

By the fourth day Moe began to wonder if he would ever get out alive. He didn't know that rescue planes had called off the search assuming he had crashed into the trees and burned. But he also didn't know that his father and a good friend, Herman Peterson, refused to give up hope.

Borrowing a plane from one of the local air services Herman began flying low over the area. He knew every tree and twig on the route, having flown it many times before. That day he spotted something different.

In the four days and five nights that Moe had been trapped on the mountainside, the weather had been kind, even though the temperature had hovered around −15°F, the ferocious winds so common to the Yukon had subsided, leaving Moe's tracks down the mountain untouched and visible from the air.

Moe was retrieved by the Canadian Air Force and soon found himself at a hospital in Edmonton, Alberta. Although his left foot was black with gangrene the doctors hoped to save it. But after a month in hospital Moe took a turn for the worst and was rushed into surgery. The next morning he woke to find both his feet had been amputated.

After having prosthesis fitted to his legs Moe didn't fly again for five years. His love for flying never waned, though. He spent much of his time at the airport until one day a pilot he knew offered to take him up. Before long Moe was working the controls and soon was a licensed pilot again.

Though the winter temperatures often drop to −30, −40 and −50°F Moe hasn't bought a pair of winter boots in more than 30 years. He goes through a lot of oxfords but ever since that accident he's had the warmest feet in the Yukon.

The tales of the Yukon are limitless. From traveling on the paddle-wheel boats that plied the Yukon River to working on a trapline, there's always a tale to tell. Some stories have spanned the years and taken on interesting new twists as the manner of the territory has changed.

There are the yarns of the dance-hall girls in the fancy hotels of Dawson City at the turn of the century. They scrambled for gold nuggets tossed to them by jovial miners. Those were the days, too, when men paid for their drinks with gold from their pokes.

But when the gold rush dwindled and the once-bustling city quieted, the hotel owners simply walked out their doors, never to return. Beds lay made, pool tables stood silent, whiskey glasses sat lonely on the huge mahogany bars.

Eventually the furniture was sold for a song and the hotels were taken down for their lumber. And so, new paydirt was struck. For with the gold and jewelry that had fallen through the floorboards during those carefree times, it is said that some men made a living by sifting through the dirt where the monuments of decadence had once stood.

»It grips you like some kinds of sinning;
It twists you from foe to a friend;
It seems it's been since the beginning;
It seems it will be to the end.«

Robert Service
THE SPELL OF THE YUKON

Notes on the authors
PHOTOGRAPHY

Brian Milne, Canada

Born in Winnipeg, Manitoba. He studied photography at Confederation College, Thunder Bay, Ontario, in 1974 and since then he has freelanced, specializing in nature/wildlife photography. His contributions to books, magazines and calendars are many and include the publications of the National Geographic Society, the National Audubon Society, the Sierra Club, as well as »Nature Canada,» Alaska Northwest Publishing, »Nature West« and many others.

Myron Wright, Alaska

Born in Charlottesville, Virginia. While in the army between 1966 and 1968, he developed an interest in photography and later, when attending college in Miami, Florida, he spent much time photographing nature and wildlife in the Everglades. He came to Alaska in 1971 as a pilot and now works for Wien Air Alaska as a first officer on Boeing 737's. Like Brian Milne, his photographs have appeared in North America's most prestigious nature and wildlife publications.

ESSAYS

Nan Elliot, Alaska

Born in California, she graduated from Williams College in Massachusetts and came to Alaska in 1973. Her activities include leading wilderness expeditions and teaching cold-water swimming in Eskimo villages. She has served as a reporter, writer and editor for newspapers, magazines and radio and television stations, and has been communications director for the Alaska Public Forum. For a number of years, she has worked in South and Central America as well as Asia and has learned much about the philosophy and lifestyles of the countries she has visited.

Lael Morgan, Alaska

She has known Alaska for almost 25 years and has traveled extensively throughout the state, concentrating on rural areas. She pursued her professional career in journalism with the »Tundra Times« of Alaska, and later with the »Los Angeles Times« in California. She then returned to Alaska under a Rockefeller Foundation Grant through the sponsorship of the Alicia Patterson Foundation. For eight years she was »roving editor« for the »Alaska Magazine.« Lael Morgan is the author of several books

published by Alaska Northwest Publishing Company and by Doubleday, New York. Since 1981, she has travelled the world on cultural assignments although, as one Alaskan publisher expressed it recently, she should forget the »fancy writing« and come back to Alaska where she belongs.

Nancy Simmerman, Alaska

An Alaskan wildlife and sports photographer as well as a writer for Alaskan and other American magazines and newspapers, she came to Alaska in the early seventies as a teacher of mathematics. After having studied photography, she now teaches this at the University of Alaska. The wilderness of Alaska is where Nancy Simmerman spends her leisure time in skiing, kayaking and other outdoor activities. At present she is working on a book on the state making use of her own skills as a photographer and writer.

Rhondda Snary, Yukon Territory

Many years ago she started out in the North as freelance writer. After having travelled throughout northern Canada, she became the editor of newspapers in Yellowknife, N.W.T. and, later, in Whitehorse. Her career has included working for the CBC in Whitehorse and writing for various Canadian and American publications. She operates a modern photographic studio in Whitehorse.

Larry Beck, Alaska

Among other things he has been appointed »Ambassador of Good Will for the State of Alaska,« because of his stage show on Alaska which he presents in many American cities during the winter time and which can be enjoyed during the rest of the year at Anchorage. Larry Beck is an acknowledged authority on the gold rush history of Alaska, and has authored books of poetry.

Andrew Hume, Yukon Territory

He came to Alaska and the Yukon in 1975, and worked as reporter and staff photographer for »The Whitehorse Star,« as well as freelancing for a number of other Canadian newspapers and magazines. His first book of which he was co-author was published in 1979. Today, his work in writing and photography is known throughout Canada.

Dick North, Yukon Territory

He arrived in the Yukon in 1963 and was engaged as reporter, columnist and editor for various newspapers and magazines in the Yukon and in Alaska. He has undertaken many expeditions throughout the Yukon and is widely known as collector of gold rush literature and photography. Dick North is the author of such well known books as »The Lost Patrol« and »The Mad Trapper of Rat River« and has been a researcher and advisor to various films and TV series that dealt with the far North. It was he who located Jack London's cabin on Henderson Creek near Dawson City for the second time.

Jim Rearden, Alaska

Resident of Alaska for more than 30 years, he has been a registered hunting guide, an outdoors writer, and a professor of wildlife management at the University of Alaska. At present he is outdoors editor for the »Alaska Magazine,« and a member of the seven-man Alaska Board of Game which sets the hunting and trapping regulations for the state. In addition, he is well known internationally as a photographer.

Lowell Thomas, Jr., Alaska

He is the son of the world-renowned traveler, author, film producer and radio newscaster, Lowell Thomas. In addition to having been state Senator and Lieutenant Governor of Alaska, Lowell Thomas Jr. is a professional pilot and operated his own flight service to wilderness areas, especially in and around Denali National Park. He accompanied his father on the famous trips to Asia and has authored himself numerous magazine articles and books, among them »Our Flight To Adventure,« the story of his and his wife's mid-fifties flight to Europe, Africa and the Middle East in their small single-engine airplane. He came to Alaska in 1958, but continued his film-making, writing and public speaking across the United States.

Space does not permit writing about the numerous other photographers who, as well as Brian Milne and Myron Wright, have contributed their art to this book.

Picture Contents

ARCTIC

Point Barrow
Barrow
PLOVER

Wainwright
POINT FRANKLIN
Peard Bay
ICY CAPE

DE LONG MOUNTAINS

CAPE LISBURNE
Cape Lisburne
Mount Hamlet 620
Tigarakpuk Mountain 1304

Kivalina
Noatak

BROOK

Mishegul Mountain 1489

BAIRD MOUNTAINS

CAPE KRUSENSTERN NATIONAL MONUMENT
CAPE KRUSENSTERN

KOBUK VALLEY NATIONAL PARK

SCHWATKA MOUNTAINS

Kotzebue
Kiana
Noorvik
Ambler
Shungnak
Kobuk

WARING MOUNTAINS

BALDWIN PENINSULA
Kiwalik
Hotham Peak
Selawik

Chukchi Sea

UNION OF SOVIET SOCIALIST REPUBLICS
UNITED STATES

Arctic Circle

Shishmaref
Shishmaref Inlet

Deering
Candle
Buckland

Cone Mountain 1372

KOTZEBUE SOUND

Wales
Brooks Mountain 883

LITTLE DIOMEDE ISLAND
Diomede

Bering Strait

Brevig Mission
Mary's Igloo
Teller

SEWARD PENINSULA

Kougarok Mountain 875

KING ISLAND

Port Clarence
POINT SPENCER

Mount Bendeleben 1137

Granite Mountain 857

Koyuk

Traverse Peak 865

Koyukuk

CAPE RODNEY

White Mountain
Moses Point
Elim
Golovin

SLEDGE ISLAND

Nome
ROCKY POINT

Christmas Mountain

Deborah Mountain 1040

Nulato
Galena

Norton Bay

CAPE DARBY

Shaktoolik
Kaltag

Norton Sound

Unalakleet

STUART ISLAND

Stebbins
Saint Michael

KAIYUH MOUNTAINS

Kotlik

Pastol Bay

Emmonak
Kwiguk
Hamilton
Alakanuk

Grayling

Ophir

Takotna
McGrath

BEAVER MOUNTAINS

Sheldon Point
North Peak 535

Anvil

Paradise Hill

Bonasila Dome

Holy Cross

Mountain Village
Saint Marys
Pilot Station
Pikas Point
Fortuna Ledge (Marshall)

Camelback Mountain 840

KUSKOKWIM

Russian Mission

Crooked Creek
Stony River

Red Devil

Cairn Mountain 1158

TAYLOR MOUNTAINS

Finn Mountain 756

Scammon Bay
Cape Romanzof

Chevak

Hooper Bay

Newtok

Kalskag
Lower Kalskag
Aniak

Whitefish Lake

Mount Hamilton 1111

Chuathbaluk

Kashegelok

Mekoryuk

NELSON ISLAND

CAPE VANCOUVER

Tununak

Toksook Bay
Nightmute
Tuntutuliak

Bethel
Akiachak
Akiak

Oscarville
Kwethluk

Napaskiak
Napakiak

KILBUCK MOUNTAINS

NUNIVAK ISLAND
Roberts Mountain 511

Chefornak

CAPE MENDENHALL
CAPE CORWIN

Eek

Kipnuk

Kongiganak
Kwigillingok

Quinhagak

Kuskokwim Bay

Goodnews Bay

AHKLUN MOUNTAINS

Togiak

Twin Hills
Wood River

Platinum

Dillingham
Aleknagik

CAPE NEWENHAM

Manokotak

Clarks Point
Ekuk

CAPE PEIRCE

HAGEMEISTER ISLAND

NUSHAGAK PENINSULA

CAPE CONSTANTINE

Bristol Bay

King Salmon

South Naknek
Naknek

Egegik

Pilot Point
Ugashik

Port Heiden

PENINSULA

STROGONOF POINT

ANIAKCHAK NATIONAL MONUMENT

Chignik Lagoon
Chignik
Chignik Lake
Chignik Bay

CASTLE CAPE

Ivanof Bay
Perryville

SEMIDI ISLANDS

Port Moller

Mount Veniaminof 2507

Nelson Lagoon

CAPE KUYUYUKAK

SUTWIK ISLAND

TUGIDAK ISLAND

PACIFIC

Moffet Point

Pavlof Volcano 2714

Cold Bay

Bechevin Bay

Morzhovoi

False Pass

Pauloff Harbor (Pavlof Harbor)

SHUMAGIN ISLANDS

NAGAI ISLAND

UNIMAK ISLAND

Shishaldin Volcano
Pogromni Volcano

Akutan

FOX ISLANDS

Dutch Harbor
Unalaska
UNALASKA ISLAND

Makushin Volcano 2036

Chernofski

Tulik Volcano
Mount Vsevidof 2109

Umnak
UMNAK ISLAND

Nikolski

ISLANDS OF THE FOUR MOUNTAINS

CARLISLE ISLAND
HERBERT ISLAND

ALEUTIAN ISLANDS

KRENITZIN ISLANDS

AKUTAN ISLAND

ANDREANOF ISLANDS

Korovin Volcano 1533
ATKA
ATKA ISLAND

ADAK ISLAND

TANAGA ISLAND

Chukchi Sea

ANADYRSKOJE PLOSKOGORJE

EKATAPSKIJ CHREBET

PEGTYMELSKIJ CHREBET

EKITYKSKIJ CHREBET

CHREBET ISKATEN

CHREBET PEKUL'NEJ

Pyrkakajveem

Gora Nuuguri 1169

Pil'gyn

Vankarem

Por'omil

Ajnguem

Nutepel'men

Enurmino
Sešan
Cegitun'

Neškan

MYS SERDCE KAMEN'

Nešan

Incoun

POLUOSTROV ČUKOTSKI

Gora Kelen'kun' 948

Uelen

Naukan
MYS MYS DEŽNEVA

Inčoun

Mečigmen
Lorino

Jandrakinot

Raupat

Providenija

Buchta Providenija

Sireniki
Uelikt
Capling

Kivak

MYS ČUKOTSKIJ

Anadyrskij Zaliv

Gora Kejki 1092

ANADYRSKAJA NIZMENNOST'

Anadyr'

Krasneno

Velkal'

Tumanskij

KORJAKSKOJE NAGORJE

Pervoje Pole

Beringovskij

Upolrivу

Meynypilgino

Buchta Ugol'naja

Buchta Gavrila

MYS NAVARIN

BERING

SEA

International Date Line

SAINT MATTHEW ISLAND
HALL ISLAND
PINNACLE ISLAND
CAPE UPRIGHT

Gambell
Savoonga

SAINT LAWRENCE ISLAND

NORTHWEST CAPE
SOUTHWEST CAPE

Northeast Cape
NORTHEAST CAPE

SOUTHEAST CAPE

SAINT PAUL ISLAND
Saint Paul Island

PRIBILOF ISLANDS

Saint George
SAINT GEORGE ISLAND

Meters | Feet
6000 | 19685
4000 | 13124
3000 | 9843
2000 | 6562
1000 | 3281
500 | 1640
200 | 656
0 | 0
Land Below Sea Level
0 | 0
200 | 656
1000 | 3281
3000 | 9843
6000 | 19685
9000 | 29520

	ENGLISH	DEUTSCH	ESPAÑOL	FRANÇAIS	PORTUGUÊS
bay	bay	Bucht	bahía	baie	baía
cape	cape	Kap	cabo	cap	cabo
island, i.	island, i.	Insel	isla	île	ilha
lake, l.	lake, l.	See	lago	lac	lago
mount, mt.	mount, mt.	Berg	monte	mont	monte
peak, pk.	peak, pk.	Gipfel	pico	cime	pico
point	point	Landspitze	punta	pointe	ponta